SLATE BLUES

SLATE BLUES

SHERI COOPER SINYKIN

LOTHROP, LEE & SHEPARD BOOKS
NEW YORK

The author wishes to thank Marc S. Cooper, for the generous use of his lyrics to "Don't Get Mad" and for his technical assistance in creating Slate and her heavy metal music scene; Vicki Berger Erwin, for providing a much-needed piece of the puzzle, friendship, and all-around support; and Judit Z. Bodnar, for her insight and for her faith.

First Edition 1 2 3 4 5 6 7 8 9 10

Library of Congress Cataloging in Publication
Sinykin, Sheri Cooper. Slate blues / by Sheri Cooper Sinykin.
p.   cm. Summary: When she finds out that the popular rock star Slate is her aunt, thirteen-year-old Reina uses the relationship to get accepted by the in-crowd at school and risks losing her best friend Nikki. ISBN 0-688-11212-9
[1. Aunts—Fiction. 2. Rock music—Fiction. 3. Popularity—Fiction. 4. Friendship—Fiction. 5. Schools—Fiction.] I. Title. PZ7.S6194S1 1993 [Fic]—dc20 92-14039 CIP AC

FOR MY BROTHER MARC,
with regrets for what was broken
and gratitude for what's being restored.

1

She was going to be late, and to make matters worse, Tuck was still pursuing her—even at the risk of being razzed by eighth graders. He knew darn well that he wasn't supposed to be in their hallway. So why did he keep scuttling after her, yammering on and tugging at her arm? Why couldn't he wait till after school?

At last Reina whirled on him, blowing her bangs off her forehead in exasperation. "Okay, already. I'll ask if anyone has an extra ticket for the concert," she said. "Now would you just go? Please?"

"You promise? You won't forget?"

"*Tuck*er," she pleaded, "I said I will and I will. Go on now. Get out of our hall. You're making me late."

"So what're they going to do? Kick you out of student council? I doubt it. What's this make? Your third year?"

Reina sighed. Getting kicked out wasn't the point. But

she hardly expected him to understand that. Like most sixth graders, Tuck would probably spend the entire first semester getting lost and being tardy and thinking nothing of it. No, she figured, there was no sense wasting time trying to explain it to her brother. Besides, knowing how he liked to bug her, she figured he'd somehow turn the whole thing into a debate and hang on like a piranha until she gave up out of annoyance or sheer exhaustion.

Sable Murphy and a couple of other girls from the pom squad were just rounding the corner from the main hall, and Reina froze. The last thing she wanted them to see was her standing there talking to a sixth grader.

"Reina, hey!" He passed his hand before her eyes. "Forget 'em. They're bimbos. Are you listening to me?" He drummed on the binder that she held in the crook of one arm, unbalancing it. It clunked to the floor, where the rings popped open, launching papers in the path of the approaching girls. "Uh-oh," he said, but made no move to collect them.

Reina clucked her tongue and glared at him. "Get out of here, will you?" She could hear the desperation in her voice and knew Tuck could, too.

"Why should I? It's a free country. I can be here if I want to be." Planting his fists on his hips, he stood there grinning, studying her as if she were some laboratory animal in a science experiment. It was absolutely sadistic, Reina thought, how he loved to make people squirm.

She tamped down her impulse to strangle him; Sable

and the others were watching, judging. There was no way she'd give any of them (Tuck included) the satisfaction of seeing her come unglued over a few lousy sheets of lined paper. Brushing past him, she stooped to reassemble her notes.

"You should've made *him* do that, Williams."

What was the point? Tuck wouldn't mind her; he never had and he never would. She was only avoiding a scene. Reina looked up into the girls' sun-kissed faces. They reeked of hair spray and of overpowering colognes. Heat flooded Reina's cheeks.

"That's okay," she said. "I can get it."

"Gonna let a sixth grader push you around?" Sable delicately poked the tip of her tongue through a pink film of gum, cocking her hip to one side. "Really, Williams, don't be such a marshmallow. Get tough, huh?" The other girls giggled.

Closing the binder, Reina slowly stood up. Did her embarrassment show? Maybe she could just laugh the whole thing off. "I-It was me," she said. "*I* dropped it. Must have been those sex ed notes, huh? Too hot to handle." Dumb. Definitely dumb.

Sable flipped her long, red hair over her shoulder and rolled her eyes. It was disgusting how green they were, Reina thought, especially since Sable swore she didn't wear tinted contacts. "Nice try, Williams, but I don't think so." She signaled to the others—Ginger, Sable's brunette clone, and blond, short-haired Carrie. "Come on, you guys. Jamey's probably sitting there, waiting for a quorum."

Reina hugged her binder to her chest, watching them go. The neon labels of their identical Flavio jeans, plainly visible on the back hip pockets, both mocked and beckoned Reina. If it weren't for Tuck, the little creep, the girls would have had no reason to tease her, might have even let her walk with them. She turned to glare at her brother, who had been mercifully silent for the last few minutes.

"Ah-ah-ah." He wagged his finger at her. "Don't say it. I'm going." With that he raced down the hall, pausing only to slam dunk an occasional imaginary basketball along the way.

Maybe he forgot to take his pill, she thought, clutching at her mother's usual excuse for Tuck's often-irritating behavior. At least she wouldn't have to deal with him again until after school—and the weekend.

Hurrying the rest of the way to Mr. J.'s room, she slipped in just as Jamey Rhoads, the student council president, was calling the meeting to order. She was grateful that the door was in the back; she'd have died a million deaths if she'd had to walk right in front of Jamey and interrupt him while he was talking.

Mr. J. glanced up from the pile of English papers he was grading at his desk as she breezed past him. For an advisor, he wasn't bad. Unlike that Mrs. Guralnik they'd had two years ago, he was a real hands-off kind of guy. Sure, he wanted them to use Robert's Rules of Order, but he was hardly the stickler she'd been. And he didn't put the kibosh on anything that wasn't his idea the way "the Growl" did, either.

But he'd really blown up at last week's meeting, said if they couldn't keep things orderly and take turns talking, he was going to resign. Judging by the quiet that had settled over the council, Reina could see that his threat was having an effect. She guessed that she wasn't the only one who preferred him to "Growlnik."

Though her best friend, Nikki Stephenson, had saved a desk up front, Reina took a less conspicuous one in the rear, just behind Carrie and across from Sable. She nibbled at her sub sandwich while Jamey plowed through the boring Old Business agenda.

"You guys are doing great today," Mr. J. said just before Jamey turned the discussion to New Business. "This parliamentary procedure stuff isn't *that* bad, now, is it?"

Some of the sixth and seventh graders mumbled replies. But this was nothing compared to the way the Growl ran meetings, Reina thought.

With a sardonic grin at the advisor, Jamey rapped his gavel for silence. "If there's no more discussion, the chair opens the floor to New Business."

Reina and Nikki both raised their hands, just as they

5

had rehearsed last night over the phone. Surely Jamey would call on one of them. But they weren't the only volunteers.

"Sable," Jamey said.

"I think we should plan something big. A dance or something. You know." She worked the room with the same hypnotic smile that had supposedly made teachers change B + s to A − s and made hungry football jocks give away the best stuff in their lunches. Agreement raced around the room.

"Mr. J.?" Jamey said. "Do we need to take a vote on this or what? Or can we just appoint a committee?"

Mr. Jankowski stroked his blond mustache and cleared his throat. "All dances have to go through the PTO, guys. I told you that right after elections, remember?"

"Like, oh-my-god," Sable whined, in that way she had of stretching *god* into two syllables. She slouched in her seat, folding her arms in disgust.

Reina thought if only she could do something to cheer Sable up, she might redeem herself for that little scene with Tuck in the hall. It never hurt to be on Sable's good side, and she'd been working on getting there since last year, when she missed making the pom squad by only a few votes. Maybe her and Nikki's idea would be just the thing. She raised her hand again, waving it at Jamey.

"Reina."

Nikki swiveled in her seat, smiling encouragement. Reina swallowed her nervousness and tried to establish eye contact with Jamey from behind her overgrown bangs.

"Maybe we could appoint a community action committee," she said.

The room was as still as a freeze-frame on the VCR. Reina blundered on, hoping to enlist some support.

"We could . . . you know . . . sponsor something to raise money for a good cause. Something big, like Sable said." She turned toward the slim redhead and smiled hopefully. "Something that would be fun and help others, too."

Sable leaned across the aisle and whispered to Carrie.

"I think that's a *great* idea," Nikki said.

"The chair didn't recognize you." Jamey banged his gavel on the lectern.

"Come on. You recognize me. I'm Nikki, remember? From Mrs. Eickert's homeroom?"

Reina and a couple of seventh graders laughed. But Jamey was playing it straight. If he only knew what a crush Nikki had on him, Reina thought, maybe he'd give her a break.

"The chair recognizes Sable."

Reina held her breath. If Sable took Reina's side, the committee was as good as formed.

"I like the idea. Comm-Comm, we could call it. Really, it's kind of like what *I* was getting at. You just didn't let me finish." She tossed Reina a little scrap of a one-sided smile. "I'd be glad to chair it, if you want."

7

"Discussion?"

Ginger and Carrie chimed in with support for Sable's leadership, and a couple of sixth and seventh graders worried aloud about whether they'd get a voice on the new committee. At last Jamey called on Nikki.

"I think Reina should chair it. After all, it was her idea."

"Maybe we should take a vote," Jamey said.

"I so move." Nikki flashed Reina a thumb's-up sign.

"Second," one of the seventh graders chimed in.

"All those in favor of Reina Williams chairing the new community action committee?"

Reina mustered enough courage to raise her hand to half-mast. It would look bad if she didn't have enough confidence to vote for herself, but then again, she didn't exactly want to tick Sable off either. Only Nikki, Tuck's friend E.J. Brooks, and a couple of seventh graders backed her.

"All those for Sable Murphy?"

Hands shot up around the room, while Sable just sat there, grinning over her landslide victory. She didn't even bother to vote.

"I *am* free to pick my own committee, aren't I?" she said. "I mean, the PTO doesn't control that, does it?"

At the back of the room, Mr. J. shook his head, amusement dancing in his eyes. "No, Sable. Pick your committee."

Rising in her chair, Sable appeared to deliberate as her

gaze took in the members of the Applewood Middle School's student council. "Mr. President," she said at last, "I choose Todd Boynton, Missy Price, Carrie Hutchings, and . . . and . . ."

She paused dramatically, looking straight at Reina.

A little knot of hope lodged in Reina's throat as she prayed to be included. Being tight with Sable and the others would turn her whole life around; she just knew it.

"And Ginger Logan," Sable said at last. "Oh. And you, of course, Mr. President."

Reina tried to hide her disappointment behind her hand. Missy Price, a member of the pom squad, was the only non-eighth grader. The others could have been chosen out of Sable's private address book; they had, collectively, about as much social conscience as that airheaded co-host on the evening version of the TV game show "That's Life."

"Madam Chairman—er, person—can we have a recommendation from your committee by next week?" Jamey asked.

"Can you guys meet after school on Wednesday?" Sable looked at her committee members, who all nodded enthusiastically. "Yes, Mr. President," she said.

"If there's no other business?"

Remembering her promise to Tuck, Reina quickly waved her hand. Jamey glanced at his watch and blew out a long breath before yielding the floor to her.

"Sorry," she said. "I'll make this quick. If anyone has an extra ticket for that concert at the Coliseum tonight, please catch me after the meeting."

"Are you kidding?" someone muttered. "That's been sold out for months."

Who cares? Reina thought. I asked. That's all I promised to do. She doubted that Mom would let Tuck go anyway, even if someone were to drop a ticket in her lap. Their mother had a thing about rock concerts, especially heavy metal. Said they exposed kids to all kinds of negative influences, not to mention harmfully high decibel levels. But Tuck could dream if he wanted to.

After Jamey adjourned the meeting, Sable and the rest of the committee gathered around him in the front of the room. Scowling in their direction, Nikki gathered up the remains of her sack lunch and hustled toward Reina. Her shoulder-length, strawberry-blond hair curled forward onto her cheeks and forehead in a new style that looked perfect. As usual, Reina thought.

"Sorry. I tried." Nikki shrugged apologetically. "I can't believe the one time I'm not late, *you* are. What happened? Long line in the cafeteria?"

"Not only that, Tuck cornered me in the hall—right in front of Madam Comm-Comm. I could have died."

Nikki lowered her voice. "Madam *Pom*-Comm is more like it."

Reina giggled. "Isn't that the truth?"

"You know they're not going to do anything but sit around planning parties," Nikki said. "Who wants to be on their dumb committee anyway?"

"*We* do. Let's be honest."

"Let's not. It's too depressing."

Tossing their trash in the basket by Mr. J.'s desk, they headed for the door. Reina glanced back over her shoulder at the new Comm-Comm members and swallowed hard. What would it take to be one of the chosen? she wondered. What could Sable possibly have against her and Nikki?

"Come on." Nikki tugged at her arm. "Just try to forget 'em."

"Right."

"Cheer up! I've got something to show you." She turned and bent forward slightly, revealing a Flavio label on the back hip pocket of her jeans. "Can you believe it?"

"I thought your Mom said—"

"The Goodwill Store," Nikki whispered. "Ten dollars. Is that great or what?"

"It's amazing!" Reina found herself wishing that *she* had the guts to wear someone else's castoffs. Didn't Nikki always manage to come up with some terrific but afford-able outfits that way? Yeah, Reina thought, but she's got a knack for combining clothes and accessories. I don't.

"Thought I'd wear them to the concert tonight. What do you think?"

Reina shrugged. How could Nikki, an otherwise sane and sensible person, get so excited about some stupid, screaming rock group?

"Reina, about the concert . . ." The warning bell shrilled on the wall overhead, and Nikki pulled Reina aside to let the others rush past them out of the room. She had guilt stamped all over her forehead. "If I'd known you wanted to go, I'd never have—"

"Not *me,* silly. Tuck. You know I hate that kind of music."

"Whew! I was afraid you were going to be mad at me for asking someone else."

"Are you kidding? You couldn't *pay* me to go."

Nikki heaved a visible sigh of relief. "I didn't think so."

A sudden crush of eighth graders sent them weaving down the hall, stopping at last in front of Nikki's locker. "Well?" Reina elbowed her friend. "Aren't you going to tell me? Who'd you finally ask? Jamey?"

"I wish." Nikki's familiar google-eyed expression made her carefully painted eyes appear even bigger. "I overheard him tell Todd that he was going with some girl from Middleton."

"So?"

"So, nothing. I'm going with"—here she lowered her voice and leaned closer to Reina—"my mom. Tell anyone and you die."

Reina tried to suppress a giggle as she crossed her heart.

"I just hope we don't run into anybody I know. What are the odds? The place'll be packed. Besides, we've got reserved seats. Sable and those guys'll be down on the floor in front of the stage, getting crushed to death."

Actually, Reina thought, it wouldn't matter too much if anyone *did* see them. Mrs. Stephenson looked and dressed young enough to pass as Nikki's big sister.

Nikki spun the dial on her lock and the shaft clicked open. "Stand back," she warned as an avalanche of papers and books descended on them both.

It was amazing how someone so together on the outside could have such a messy locker, not to mention a messy room, Reina thought as she stooped to help retrieve the fallen texts.

Handing them up, she fought back a squirmy feeling in the pit of her stomach. She didn't envy Nikki the concert, but it *was* kind of neat how open-minded Mrs. Stephenson was. She not only looked like Nikki's sister, she acted like one, too. Maybe that explained Reina's pangs; she'd have given anything for a sister. As it was, her own mother professed to know with absolute certainty what was right for herself, Reina, and everyone else in the world. Not exactly open-minded, Reina thought glumly. And not exactly great substitute-sister material either.

"Well," she said, once Nikki had selected her books and slammed the door on the others, "you guys have fun tonight."

"We will. Mom's cool. Cooler than Tuck, no offense."

"Hey," Reina said, raising one hand, "none taken."

Out of the corner of her eye she spied a glimpse of Sable's coppery hair. Despite the din of slamming lockers and shuffling feet, the girl's laughter hung in the air, distinctive as harpsichord music.

"Come on," Reina said.

"Do I look okay? How's my scarf?"

Reina fussed with the artistically draped triangle, then withdrew her hands in dismay. Nikki could have done better with her eyes closed. "It's fine. Come on. I think we can catch her. Maybe she'll at least *listen* to our ideas."

2

Reina awoke at eight o'clock the next morning to the screech of heavy metal music blaring from her clock radio. Her heartbeat pounded against her chest as she leaped up to silence it. *"Tucker!"* she yelled, banging on the wall. "That wasn't funny, you hear? It's Saturday. I wanted to sleep in."

She was sure that he was next door in his room, laughing his head off, plotting new ways to bug her. What would he think of next?

"Tuck?" Silence. "You put that junk on my radio again and you're in big trouble." God, now he had her talking to walls.

Catching sight of her scowling reflection in the mirror over the dresser, she fussed in vain with her long, frizzy bangs. Tuck was the least of her problems, she thought as she finger combed dark, shoulder-length hair away

15

from her face, the way she'd worn it for the past three years. Maybe she should get it straightened. Or cut. Something—anything!—to make her look older, better. More like the girls in Pom-Comm. She bet Nikki would know what to do with it, but there was no way she dared call her until at least ten. Nikki'd kill her, especially since she'd been up late at that dumb rock concert.

Feet pummeled up the stairs and down the hall outside her room, accompanied by shrieks and howls. Someone pounded on her door. "Reina, let me in! Save me!"

Reina rolled her eyes, cracking the door just wide enough to admit her four-year-old brother, Brady. "What's that big bully doing to you now?" she asked, bending over to examine him for cuts or bruises. His pudgy cheeks were red as if from a recent tweaking.

"Tuck did a 'baby face' on me again. I tell him I don't like it, but he does it anyway." Brady stuck out his lower lip and regarded her with doleful eyes.

Reina ran her fingers through his dark cap of wiry hair; it felt just like her own. "Tuck can be a real buttso sometimes, can't he?"

"Yeah." Brady nodded solemnly. "He's a buttso all right."

Reina's door slammed open against the closet. Tuck sprang into the room as if he were a four-and-a-half-foot-tall frog. Brady screamed and cowered behind Reina, clinging to her nightgown.

"I heard that," Tuck said. "I am *not* a buttso."

Reina mustered her most authoritative tone. "Get out of here. Go do something besides bugging everybody."

"What did I do, huh? You guys blame me for everything."

"That's because you *do* everything," Reina said. "And next time you put that heavy metal noise on my radio and set it to go off at the crack of dawn, I'm going to . . ." She struggled to find the right consequence. "Well, I don't know what I'll do. But you won't like it, that's for sure."

Tuck stood there, chewing on the inside of his cheek, his straight blond hair sticking out like exclamation marks. His eyes were moss-green slits. "You're so square, Reina," he said. "I swear you're like a clone of Mom. Straight out of the sixties."

Reina stole a guilty look at the Beach Boys poster her mother had given her. It was taped to the wall above the headboard of her white canopy bed. She jutted out her chin. "So what if I am? You saying there's something wrong with Mom?"

Tuck shrugged. "You think *she'd* make Pom-Comm? *I* don't."

Reina's cheeks burned. How could he know her and Nikki's pet name for the new committee unless he'd been eavesdropping on them yesterday after school? "Just get out of here," she said, steering him toward the door. "I told you before. And I'm going to tell Mom if you don't leave us alone."

Tuck kicked up to a handstand in the doorway and

17

rolled out into the hall. "She's talking long distance. To Dad. Better not bother her."

Reina closed the door and locked it. Brady hopped onto her unmade bed and began playing with the old stuffed lamb she still slept with every night.

"And leave Chopsie alone," she snapped.

A light went out in Brady's eyes, and she wished at once that she could recall the words. But it was too late. He slunk off the bed and toward the door, his head bent low. "Thanks for saving me, Reina," he said without looking at her.

Reina swallowed the lump in her throat. "I'm sorry, Brade. I didn't mean to jump on you. Here. You wanna play with him?" She held out the limp animal, but Brady shook his head and slipped out of the room.

Relocking the door, she cradled Chopsie and flopped onto her bed. If only Tucker weren't such a brat, if only my hair weren't such a mess, if only I were on Pom-Comm, if only I had a sister who'd understand, then I'd be happy, she thought. Laying the stuffed lamb aside, she pulled a dog-eared notebook from under her mattress and worked the stubby pencil free from its spiral binding.

"September 26th," she wrote. "Brothers are what God made to keep the world from running smoothly. They wake you up when you want to sleep, and always, *always* forget to lift the toilet seat when they go. They put you down and listen in on the phone and touch your things.

Brothers stink." So why, she wondered, did she feel so guilty for getting mad at them?

She closed the notebook and slid it back into hiding. Then she snapped a Beach Boys cassette into her tape player and turned up the volume. As the sweet falsetto rose to fill the room, her mood lightened. Grabbing her deodorant stick off her dresser, she held it to her mouth and pretended it was a microphone.

The harmony caught her in its web. She tossed her head, making believe her hair gleamed and bounced just the way the shampoo commercials promised. Then she faced the mirror and belted out the lyrics in a powerful alto voice. Her dream-reflection grinned an Ultra-Brite smile and tossed Preference hair, spun gold in color. Her nose, no longer wide and pudgy like Brady's and Dad's, was narrow with the slightest upturn like Mom's and Tuck's. When she danced during the music bridge, her moves rivaled Sable Murphy's, and *she* was now the Pom-Comm chair. As the ballad dissolved into silence, Reina bowed before her mirror-audience, then tossed the deodorant stick into her other hand, catching it with a flourish.

The pace picked up during the next song, an old surfing tune. She wiggled her hips in time to the drums, singing the lyrics into the pretend microphone. Something popped behind her. Tuck burst into the room.

"Aha! Gotcha!" he said, clicking a photo with an imaginary camera. "Wait till I tell E.J."

19

Her privacy violated, Reina hugged herself as if she were naked. Anger worked its way up from the pit of her stomach. She ached to bean him with the deodorant. But with her arm and his luck, she'd probably put a dent in the wall instead.

"You tell Big Mouth Brooks and I'll rip up your sugar-packet collection. That is, unless you've already eaten it," she said. "You're so hyper all the time, I wouldn't be surprised."

"Very funny. You know I've got attention deficit. It's not *my* fault." But Tuck sobered at her threat. "Bet you don't even know where I keep it anymore, so there."

"All I have to do is follow the trail of ants."

"Ha! Ha! Very funny," Tuck repeated, cocking his head as if to welcome her verbal jabs.

"When Daddy comes back from his trip," Reina said, "I'm going to make him get me a new lock. One that even *you* can't pop."

Tuck rubbed his hands together, his eyes gleaming. "What does that give me? A month of merry pop-ins?" He doubled over with laughter at his own stupid joke.

"Why don't you act your age, not your nonexistent IQ? Get out of here!" Reina said through gritted teeth. "I mean it!" When Tuck did not go, she shoved him into the hall and slammed the door. "And stay out!"

With her back pressed against the door, she slid down into the thick pile of her blue-gray carpet. As she drew up her knees and hugged them, she blinked back sudden tears. Tuck's telling E.J. Brooks would be like announcing it over the school's intercom. Sable and the others would know she was weird for sure. She might as well transfer out right now, because her life at A.M.S. would be as good as over.

"Reina, breakfast," Mom called from downstairs.

Reina sniffed, wiped her cheeks with the back of her hand, and grabbed her robe. "Coming."

She managed a smile for her mother as she took her place at the table. Tuck and Brady already had disassembled *The Capital Times,* clothing the polished oak with newsprint. "Do you guys mind?" she said, clearing a space for the plate of French toast that Mom had handed her.

Brady folded up the comics and tucked a paper napkin into his T-shirt. But Tuck, lost in the *Weekender* section, gave no indication that he'd even heard her. "Where do they print the reviews?" he asked.

"Books or records?" Mom replied, serving Brady his breakfast and placing a square orange pill in front of Tuck.

"Shows. I mean, concerts. Never mind. I found 'em."

"Tucker, take your pill please," Mom said.

"I will."

"Now."

Tucker pursed his lips and glared up at Mom. "I don't want it. I hate it. Tastes terrible."

"Then learn to swallow it," Mom said. "Please? No

21

arguments this morning, okay?" She sighed. "It's been about a month since school started. You should be up to your normal dose by now."

"Why?"

"Because it helps you concentrate. Don't tell me it doesn't."

"Yeah, yeah," Tuck said. "Helps *you*, that's who it helps." He grudgingly placed the pill in his mouth and crunched down. After several moments of exaggerated chewing, he opened wide and stuck out his tongue. "Satisfied?"

Mom simply nodded, and Reina bit into her French toast. At least her stomach wasn't in knots. Most mornings, when Tuck and Mom *really* got into it about his medication, Reina could hardly eat.

"Here it is. All right!" Tuck jerked the newspaper off the table and held it up to his face. "Have you talked to Nikki?" he asked.

"Not today." Reina cut Brady's bread into small pieces and sprinkled them with powdered sugar.

"Amazing! You ought to call her, get the inside information," Tuck said, still barricaded behind the newspaper. "Says here Slate collapsed on stage at the Coliseum. Had to be rushed to Meriter Hospital."

"Who's Slate?" Reina asked, as if she really cared.

"Who's Slate? *Who's Slate?*" Tuck slapped the paper down and stared at Reina as if she'd time-traveled from another century. "The star. The big banana. The one

I wanted you to get me a ticket to. Jeez, Reina. I can't believe you. I bet even Mom's heard of Slate, right, Mom?"

"Hmmm?" Mom turned off the water she'd been running in the sink. "What did you say?"

Tuck shook his head in exasperation. "We were talking about Slate. The rock star, you know? She collapsed last night, right in the middle of her concert. And Reina acts like she's never even heard of her."

Mom pinched her lips together and blinked quickly. "May I?" she said, taking the newspaper from Tuck. As she scanned the article, her eyes began to water. She rescued a wadded tissue from her apron pocket and dabbed at the corners. "Damn her," she said, her voice only a whisper. "Damn her anyway."

Brady's jaw dropped; Mom rarely swore. Reina motioned for him to keep quiet as she stood up, crossed to her mother's side, and slipped her arm around her shoulder.

"What's with *her?*" Tuck said, winding his finger in circles by his head.

"Shush!" Reina glared at her brother. "Can't you see she's upset?"

"Jeez. What's the big deal? All I said was Slate collapsed. It's not like she died or anything."

Mom fumbled through the telephone book. Her hands were shaking. Reina rubbed her back. "Mom, what's wrong?" she said. "You look like you've seen a ghost."

Mom mustered a lopsided grin as she slapped the book shut and reached for the telephone. "Maybe I have," she said, holding up one finger for silence. "Yes, operator. I need the number for Meriter Hospital. Patient information."

3

Reina held her breath as Mom dialed the hospital. Why in the world would she be calling some big-deal rock star?

"*Moth*-er," Tuck said, his hands on his hips. "What are you doing?"

Mom wagged her finger for silence. "May I please have Amanda Slate's room?" she said into the receiver.

"A-*man*-da." Small bits of French toast dropped out of Brady's mouth as he spoke. "I have a girl in my class named A-*man*-da."

"Brady, will you quit that?" Tucker rolled his eyes. "Jeez, Mom. I don't believe you're—"

Reina cut him off with a snap of her fingers. How could she hear what Mom was saying with her brothers shooting off their mouths?

"Not accepting calls. I understand," Mom said. "But

I'm sure she'll see me. Isn't there a list of approved visitors or something? Would you check with her security people? Yes. I am."

I am *what*? Reina wondered.

"My name's Emily Williams," Mom said after a long pause. "It's there? Thanks so much."

"This is unbelievable!" Tuck said. "She's on Slate's list, right? She's going to visit her. Or am I hearing things?" He pranced around the kitchen, punching the air with his fists. "All right, Mom! Way to go!"

Reina nailed him with a steely glare. "Will you just be quiet and give her a break?"

She looked over her mother's shoulder as Mom scribbled a room number and some times on the back of an envelope. Why would Mom want to visit a rock star, a complete stranger? Surely not to impress Tuck. It didn't make any sense unless . . . Amanda Slate *wasn't* a stranger. What if she was an old friend, someone from Mom's past? College, maybe. Or her old neighborhood.

Reina repeated the name over and over to herself, wondering why it rolled so easily off her tongue. Amanda. A-*man*-da. Once, at Christmas, they'd gotten what appeared to be a box of Swiss Colony cheese that said "Season's Greetings from Aunty Mandy" on the packing label. Mom had told the UPS guy to send it back, that she didn't know anyone by that name. And that night she and Dad had had a heated debate about why someone in Los

Angeles would send a gift of cheese (of all things!) to Wisconsin, America's Dairyland.

Aunty Mandy? Reina stared at her mother, trying to conjure up the family tree she'd drawn in sixth grade. Was that Mom's sister's name, the one she never wanted to talk about? What had Reina written in the circle next to Emily Ann Brady? She'd had to squeeze it in because it was so long, and she never had been satisfied with the way it looked. Miranda Marie . . . Amanda Marie . . . something like that. She wished she could remember exactly.

Reina turned the names over in her mind. Which was it? Miranda or Amanda? The two were so similar, so easy to confuse. But if her aunt had signed the card Mandy, then her name *had* to be Amanda, right? Could she and this Amanda Slate person be one and the same?

As Mom hung up the phone, Reina touched her arm and whispered, "She's your sister, isn't she? The one you never talk about."

Mom eyed the floor, gave a quick nod.

An unexpected storm of emotions whirled up within Reina: excitement, confusion, anger. "Our aunt's a famous rock star, and you never even told us?" she said, still keeping her voice low so that Tuck wouldn't overhear and go crazy. "I don't get it."

"I have my reasons, Reina. Trust me."

Tuck came dancing over. "Well? Well? Did you fix it so we can visit Slate?"

27

"No, Tucker."

"But I heard you say—"

"Never mind what you heard," she said. "It's none of your business."

"Mo-om! We're talking about *Slate* here. Any kid would kill to meet her. And you're on her list."

"Back off," Reina said. "It's none of your business."

"None of your business," Brady echoed, carrying his plate to the sink. "Tell me, Reina. What's the business?"

"Not now, Brady." Reina turned to her mother. Mom was rubbing worry lines from her forehead, her expression pained. Gray strands, salted through her short blonde hair, caught the fluorescent light and kept it. They seemed to age her before Reina's eyes. Now was definitely not the time to press the issue about Aunt Amanda.

"You want me to watch the boys so you can go?" Reina said.

"I guess I really should, shouldn't I?"

Reina nodded. Though she tried hard not to judge her mother, it was all she could do to keep from blurting her thoughts. Reina had dreamed of having a sister for as long as she could remember. And Mom was acting like she didn't even care about hers! "Trust me," Mom had said. "I have my reasons." Whatever they were, Reina thought, they'd better be good. Grudgingly, she held her tongue.

"Grandma and Grandpa would want me to go," Mom said, as if still trying to talk herself into the visit. "They'd roll over in their graves if Amanda was bad off and I didn't at least see her."

Reina bit her lip, rubbing away goose bumps that suddenly pebbled her arms. It had been six years—almost half her life—since Grandma and Grandpa Brady had died, one right after the other, practically. Still, the ache persisted.

"Go," Reina said. "Don't worry about a thing. We'll be fine."

"Thanks, honey. Sometimes I don't know what I'd do without you."

"If you're going to see Slate," Tuck said, "then I'm going, too. What's the deal? You know her from school or something?"

Mom heaved a great sigh and studied the ceiling for a long moment. Tucker and Brady looked up, too, then burst into giggles.

"You guys! Just cool it, will you?" Maybe, Reina thought, Mom wouldn't tell them. It could be their little secret, girls only. It'd serve her brothers right for goofing around.

"What?" Tuck demanded. "What were you going to say?"

"Nothing. Never mind." Mom fumbled through her purse for her car keys. "It wasn't important." She turned to Reina. "I won't be gone any longer than I have to." She donned a pair of reflector sunglasses, hiding her lack of makeup.

"Want me to do your eyes real quick?" Reina offered. Besides highlighting the blue of Mom's eyes, she would smudge the eyeliner for sultry effect as Nikki had shown her.

Mom shook her head. "What's the point?"

Reina shrugged. Mom wasn't even trying, didn't care *how* she looked. What was the matter with her anyway? "Well," she said, following her mother down the hall, "I hope she's okay."

"Knowing her, she probably is." Mom brushed Reina's hair back off her face. A strange faraway look veiled her eyes. At last she shook free of her thoughts. "Nah, you're much prettier than Mandy ever was." She kissed Reina quickly on the cheek, and then she was gone.

Reina touched her hand to the spot where her mother's lips had been. Me, pretty? Mom's hardly unbiased. She only said that because she's grateful I'm watching the boys for her. Beats paying me by the hour, she thought. Besides, if Amanda Slate looked as freaky as the rest of those mangy heavy metal creeps, Mom's comparison was hardly a compliment. Maybe Nikki would have a picture of her in one of those rock magazines she insisted on buying.

Reina could hear Brady and Tuck wrestling in the family room, screaming and laughing in the same breath. Something was going to get broken. Either that or someone would get hurt. Probably Brady.

"You guys settle down," she called, "and I won't make you use points to watch TV."

"Tuck! Hey, Tucker! Reina says free TV."

Her brothers thundered toward her down the hall. "Mom say you could?" Tucker asked, suspicious. "I'm not losing forty points an hour for *cartoons*." He spat out the last word with disdain, but Brady seemed not to notice.

"It's okay, right, Reina? If I turn it on, you won't take away points?"

Reina shook her head. "But you've got to sit on separate chairs and no fooling around."

"We won't," Brady said, promising for them both.

"Well, okay then." Reina backed toward the stairs. "I'm going up to call Nikki."

After borrowing the cordless telephone from her parents' room and closing her door, she dialed the Stephensons' house. As she waited for Nikki to answer, she made her bed.

"You'll never guess what happened last night," Nikki said. "Never in a million skillion years. You want to guess, or should I tell? Let me tell, okay?"

Reina laughed. There was no way to stop Nikki, once she got started. "Go ahead, but I bet I already know."

"How could you? You're kidding me, right? Bet you don't even remember where I—"

"You went to see Slate at the Coliseum. And she

collapsed on stage. And you'll never guess what."

"What?"

"Slate's my aunt."

"No way. You're kidding me, right?"

"I'm not. I just found out a few minutes ago. Weird, huh?"

"I can't believe it. You must be going crazy. Slate is your aunt? Amazing! But why didn't you know? I mean . . . your *aunt*? Really?"

"Really." Reina laughed. Nikki seemed much more excited about the news than Reina herself did. "I guess they must have had a fight or something. I don't know. Mom says she has her reasons for not telling us."

"Incredible!" Nikki fell silent for a long moment. "Don't you realize how great this is?"

"Uh . . . no."

"Just think about it. What do you suppose Madam Pom-Comm will do when she finds out you're—shall we say—well-connected? I'm serious, Williams. This could turn everything around for us. Everything."

Reina rearranged the pink and lavendar throw pillows on her bed, then sat down at her desk. Nikki had lost her. Totally. What could Slate possibly have to do with Pom-Comm? "You're crazy," she said. "So she's my aunt. I don't even know her."

"But you can change that, can't you? Go to the hospital. Take her some flowers or—no, wait. I've got a better idea. You tell the kids at school who she is and have everyone sign a big, humongous card. Then bring *that* to the hospital. Sable and those guys will be begging to go along and—voilà!—you're in."

"Not bad."

"Not bad? Is that all you can say? If you ask me, it's inspired. Pure genius."

"Wait a minute, Nikki. Hold on, will you?" Reina turned around slowly in her chair and stared at the door. A shadow moved beneath it. *"Tucker!"* She sprang forward and, as she did, her brother flung the door open, smacking her in the forehead. She howled, more in anger than in pain.

Tucker planted himself in the doorway, his arms folded across his chest. "What do you mean, not telling me, huh? I heard every word you said."

Reina rubbed her forehead. The mirror revealed a red stripe above her left eye. "I'm on the phone," she said evenly. "Go away."

"Oh, no you don't. You're not getting rid of me that easy."

Reina picked up the phone, turning her back on Tucker. "Nikki? I've gotta go. I'm baby-sitting, and Tuck's bratting out on me."

Nikki cursed softly. "Why can't he just leave you alone? He never lets up, does he?"

"You got that right."

"Well, anyway . . ." Nikki's tone left a trail of disappointment. "I've got to sit the twins tonight so Mom and

Dad can go to some policeman's ball or something. Call me later, okay?"

"I will." Reina brushed past her brother to replace the telephone in her parents' room. When she returned, she was annoyed—but somehow not surprised—to see Tuck still standing in her doorway. "What are *you* looking at?" she said.

"You, that's who. World's weirdest sister. Why didn't you tell me Slate is our aunt? Jeez, E.J.'s going to freak out when he hears that I met Slate. In the flesh."

"You didn't meet her," Reina said.

"Not yet. But I'm going to. How much is bus fare? Forty-five cents?" Without waiting for her reply, he headed into his room.

Reina chased after him. "Just where do you think you're going?"

Tucker emerged from his closet, rattling a handful of coins, and inspected her forehead, his face just inches from hers. "Same place you are. Big bump you've got there, Reina. Better have someone at the hospital look at it."

Reina's jaw dropped. "We're *not* going to the hospital," she said, "so you can put that away."

Tucker ignored her. He kicked a pile of clothes into his closet and scooted past her into the hall. As he thumped down the stairs, he called ahead to Brady, "How'd you like to take a bus ride? How'd you like to meet Aunty Slate?"

Reina flung off her bathrobe in a panic and raced into her room. "Brady?" she yelled. "Don't you dare go with him, you hear?" There was no reply. "Brady Williams! You are not to go out that door!"

Her fingers fumbled with the pearly buttons on her nightgown. Tucker wouldn't go, would he? Wriggling into a pair of jeans and a "Don't Worry, Be Happy" T-shirt, she grabbed her bus pass off her dresser and began searching for her sandals.

"Tucker? Brade? You'd better stay right there."

Down on her hands and knees, she groped in vain among the dust ruffles of her white eyelet bedspread until the unmistakable slam of the front door propelled her to her feet.

Reina rested her temple against the city bus's window, letting the air conditioning blast her squarely in the face. Brady tugged at her T-shirt. "Reina," he said, "are you still mad? Maybe a hug will help."

He wrapped his arms around her middle, pressed his cheek against her chest. Reina, self-conscious, wiggled free of his embrace. She started to bite at a hangnail, then remembered that that was a habit she was trying to break. What was she going to say to Mom when they showed up at the hospital? That Tuck had kidnapped her? God, he was a pain. How did he manipulate her into doing these things?

"When do we get off? Do I ding the bell yet or what?" Tuck said.

"You tell me, Mr. Know-It-All."

36

"Reina, *tell* him," Brady said, his eyes like black holes. "I don't want to be lost without Mama."

Reina patted his head, sudden love for him welling up inside her. "Don't worry. We're not lost. And even if we were, I'd take care of you."

"Okay, I'm pulling it," Tuck said. Before Reina could stop him, he had tugged on the cord five times.

An elderly woman with a shopping cart glared at him from across the aisle. "Where's your mama at?" she said.

"The hospital," Tuck said solemnly. "We're going to see her right now."

The woman's eyes lit up. A smile creased her cheeks. "New baby?"

Tuck nodded, and Reina elbowed him in the ribs. "We're going to visit our aunt," she said, wondering why it should bother her to lie even to a stranger. If imagining them visiting a new brother or sister made the old lady happy, why couldn't Reina just keep her big mouth shut?

"*I'm* the baby," Brady said, showing off his dimples. "Wanna see my loose tooth?"

Reina rolled her eyes in silent apology. But sensing that the woman actually welcomed Brady's attention, she let him babble on until they reached their stop at the corner of Park Street and Regent. Tuck bounded off the bus and down the block toward the hospital's main entrance. Reina hurried after him, clutching Brady's hand.

By the time they reached the patient information desk,

Tuck had already attracted a security guard. "I'm not just any kid," her brother was saying. "I'm her nephew. Tucker Williams. Call up there and see for yourself. Have 'em check the list."

The officer, a young, wormy-looking guy with greasy blond hair and black-framed glasses, looked questioningly at Reina. "You with him?" She nodded. "Is that true—Slate's his aunt?"

"Yes," Reina said, "but she wouldn't recognize my brother. I mean, we've never exactly met."

"Hmmmph. Sounds like a good story if you ask me."

Tuck telegraphed his irritation to Reina as if to say "Shut up and let me do the talking." She bristled at the unspoken suggestion. Tuck might think he was as smart as a grown-up, but he *was* only eleven, and she was in charge here, not he.

"My sister hurt her head," Tuck said, "and since our mother's here, we thought . . . Well, you wouldn't want her to keel over right here in the lobby, would you?"

Reina writhed under the officer's scrutiny of her forehead. "You *do* got a goose egg there," he admitted. "Well, write out your names and let me make a couple of calls, see what her security guy says. You got some kind of I.D.?"

Reina patted down her pockets, turning up only her bus pass and house keys.

"Sorry."

"Here," Tuck said, shoving at the officer a hard plastic card with blue stripes. "Library card'll work."

Reina grudgingly admired Tuck's confidence, the way he just assumed they were going to get past the guard.

The officer fingered the card hesitantly. "We generally like a picture I.D., a driver's license. But then, you're a little young for that."

"This'll work," Tuck repeated.

The guy shrugged and disappeared into his office for several minutes. At last he emerged, a confirming grin mirroring Tuck's hopeful one. "Guess you're for real. Names're on the list. All three of 'em. But I gotta take you up there myself."

Tuck's eyes glowed green with his victory. He nudged Reina pointedly and fell in behind the security guard.

As they awaited an elevator, Brady yanked on Reina's hand. "I've gotta go potty," he whispered.

Reina scanned the hall. There probably was a bathroom around someplace, she thought. But if she took Brady, then Tuck would be on the loose (there was no way *he'd* go into the women's restroom) and she didn't like that idea at all. "Can you wait till we get upstairs?" she said.

Brady shrugged. "I guess so."

"Good." The ding of the elevator bell made her heart beat faster. Mom was never going to trust her with anything again after a stunt like this. Reina imagined the look of disappointment in her mother's eyes, and her stomach turned flip-flops. Was it too much to hope for that she'd already come and gone?

The guard led them down the starched-white halls of Seven Tower, and stopped to chat with another officer in front of a door bearing the warning ALL VISITORS MUST REPORT TO THE NURSE'S STATION. "You three wait here," he said. "I've still got to clear it with the nurse."

He walked away in a jangle of keys. With the private guard's attention momentarily diverted to his clipboard, Tuck tried to inch past. Reina grabbed her brother's arm the same instant the guard did; she pulled him aside. "Would you stop that? You're going to get us in trouble. What if she OD'd or something?" she said. "I'm telling you, we shouldn't be here."

"Slate wouldn't do drugs." Tuck eyed her with scorn. "Don't be dumb. Just 'cause she's a rock star, doesn't mean she's a junkie."

"What do you know about it?" Reina said. "You're just a kid."

"So what? I can read *Metal Mania*, can't I? I can watch MTV."

"That's about all you can do," Reina muttered.

Brady tapped her hand. "Gotta go bad," he said, his eyes pleading.

At Reina's request, the guard pointed out a men's restroom down the hall. "Tuck, take him, will you?" she said. "And stay there till he's done, in case he can't open the door."

Tuck grumbled but, amazingly, did as he was told. They were still in there when the officer returned and said she could go in. The other guard noted something on his clipboard but did not move from his protective stance in front of the door.

"It's okay," her officer-escort said. "The nurse already called down here, and Slate said to let her in."

The guard nodded abruptly and stepped aside. Reina mustered her courage and opened the door.

A lake view, flooded with sunshine and vases of roses, pots of chrysanthemums, and baskets of violets, dominated the private room. A curtain was drawn partway around the bed. From behind it came murmured voices.

The man's was like velvet, soft and smooth. "Okay, babe, be cool now," he said. "We'll hang in at the Sheraton till you let us know what's going down."

Reina turned to go, but the man flung open the curtain and the grating of metal-on-metal froze her in place. "What are you looking for?" he said.

Reina swallowed hard. His blue eyes riveted her words to the back of her throat. Despite his long blond hair, despite three earrings and an unshaven face, he was gorgeous, absolutely. "My . . . my . . . mother," Reina managed at last, her voice hoarse. "She was supposed to be here."

41

He made a sweeping gesture of the room. "There's no mother here." A soft rustling of sheets made him look over his shoulder. "Sorry," he said to the person in the bed. "I forgot, okay?"

Reina strained to see beyond him, but could not. "My mom . . . she's . . . Slate's sister," she said.

The man laughed. Reina could not take her eyes off the zillions of slashes in his whitewashed jeans. "That's the best one yet, hey, Slate?"

The woman coughed as if to clear her throat, but only a harsh whisper came out: "I want to see her, Razor. Go on now. Leave us alone."

Razor raised one eyebrow. "You sure? Looks like a groupie to me. Maybe I'd better stick around." His grin could have melted the North Pole.

The woman snapped her fingers. "I said, go on."

Razor shrugged. "Okay, okay. See you around, babe," he said, looking straight at Reina, but obviously talking to Slate.

Reina closed her eyes, but could feel his warmth, could smell the leather of his vest, as he brushed past her. She dared not look at what the cuts in his jeans might reveal from behind.

"Come on over here, sweetie," the woman rasped. "I can't see without my contacts."

Reina drew closer. Her breath caught at the sight of this pale woman—her aunt—whose hair flowed over the sheets like vats of spilled ink. Even sick, she was breathtaking, with eyes the color of wood violets, naturally, without colored contacts. "I'm—"

"Reina, right?" Slate smiled. "I always loved that name. Even before your mother picked it out for you."

Reina shifted her weight, uncomfortable at Slate's reference to Mom. "Where . . . where is she, anyway?"

Slate's shoulders rose and fell almost imperceptibly. "Went for some coffee. Or to make a phone call. Might even be talking to my doctors for all I know. That's big sisters for you, always taking charge."

"I wouldn't know," Reina said, wishing for the eighty-eleventh time that she had one.

Slate laughed. "Guess I'll have to ask your brothers about that now, won't I?"

Her brothers! "Oh, God! I've got to go find them!"

"Come back when you do," Slate said. "I'll be here."

Reina flung open the door. There was no sign of either of them in the hall. She raced down to the men's restroom and paused outside, knocking lightly at last. She was taken aback when Razor opened the door.

Again, the raised eyebrow, the half smile. "We've got to stop meeting like this, love," he said.

Beyond him she could see Brady standing beneath the blow dryer and Tuck blotting Brady's pants with a paper towel. "My brothers." She shrugged apologetically. "They almost done?"

"Almost," he said. "Little guy had an accident. And the big one darn near gave him a bath in the sink."

43

"Ohhh," Reina wailed, imagining Brady's humiliation.

"Hey, Reina!" Tuck called. "Betcha don't know who *you're* talking to."

Sudden warmth bathed her cheeks. "Of course I do," she said, avoiding the cobalt eyes. "Razor."

"Razor who?" Tuck persisted. "What does he play?"

Reina could hardly breathe, wished the earth would open up and swallow her whole. Razor grinned and extended his hand. "Razor Jamison. Drums." Reina accepted his rescue; his touch sent a chill skittering down her spine.

"Get his autograph, Reina. I did," Tuck said.

She wished she could shove a roll of toilet paper down the kid's throat. "I-I don't have any . . . paper," she said.

"That's okay. Paper gets lost too easy anyway." She looked away as Razor searched his slashed pants' pockets. Was he even wearing underwear? At last he brandished a pen and, without invitation, squatted and scribbled his name on her jeans, just above the knee.

Reina was too stunned to move or to speak.

"Wait till Pom-Comm sees *that,*" Tuck said, giving Razor the A-OK sign.

Tuck had gone too far this time. Any judge or jury would agree. But Reina suppressed the urge to charge past Razor and drown her brother in the toilet. Even if Razor was just a creepy long-haired drummer, she'd be darned if Tuck would get the better of her in front of him. Her brother's murder would have to wait.

"I'll be in Slate's room," she said, a tight rein on her anger. "You two come in when Brady's dry."

"Hey, no fair," Tuck protested, blotting his brother's pants with renewed energy. He was probably guilt-ridden for soaking him in the sink in the first place. But more likely, he was only afraid he'd miss something by dallying.

"I'm sorry, Reina," Brady said. "I told you I had to go bad."

Reina sighed. "It's okay, Brade. I'm not mad at you."

Razor stood there, grinning, his thumbs hooked on what was left of his pockets. Reina's cheeks went hot again. "You're *welcome*," he said pointedly.

What? Oh, yeah. The autograph. She nodded, and backed down the hall. "Thanks," she said. "I meant to say it before. Really."

As she pushed Slate's door open, her mother's voice filled the private room. "I know just what you're doing, Amanda. And it's not going to work."

"You're paranoid, Emmy, you know that? You'd think that after all these years we could bury the hatchet. You're . . ." Slate paused, coughed weakly. "You're all the family I've got."

"Whose fault is that?" Mom said. The bitter edge in her voice made Reina wince. "You know what Mama used to say: 'You made your bed, now lie in it.' Anyone can cough and act weak. I wouldn't put it past you to have faked your so-called collapse."

"Now why would I do a thing like that?"

"You tell me. You want something, don't you? Come on, out with it."

Slate's sigh stirred Reina's compassion. "What did I ever do to hurt *you?*" she asked at last. "Really, Em. I want to know."

"It doesn't matter," Mom said. "Not anymore."

"Why don't I believe that?"

Reina cleared her throat to announce her presence, steeling herself for Mom's reaction. Whatever, she thought, it would beat listening to her and Slate tear each other apart.

"Reina, sweetie, come on in." Slate whirred the head of her bed into action, fussed with her hair as she sat up to greet her visitor.

Mom spun about, her eyebrows hiking up in her surprise. "What are *you* doing here?" she demanded.

5

Reina touched the lump on her forehead and thought about using Tuck's excuse but rejected it. She bit her lip and sighed. "Tucker talked me into it," she said. "I know, I know. Don't say it. He's only eleven, and I'm thirteen; I should know what's right and wrong. But you know how he is, Mom."

Her mother pursed her lips, said nothing. Reina knew that look. It usually masked an angry lecture that Mom didn't feel she could unleash at that moment. But Reina was sure to hear it later. Boy, would she.

"So," Mom said, "have you two met?"

Reina nodded. "But I don't know what to call you," she said, turning to her aunt. "Aunty Mandy sounds sort of . . ." She trailed off, not wanting to hurt her aunt's feelings.

Slate's full lips edged upward. "You're right." Reina

had to listen hard to hear her. That argument with Mom must have really stressed what was left of her voice. "I hated calling our aunt 'Cookie' when I was fifteen, remember, Em?"

"Reina's *not* fifteen."

"Could have fooled me," Slate said with a wink. Reina slouched in embarrassment, wishing her breasts weren't quite so obvious in this T-shirt. "How about calling me Aunt Slate?"

Mom glared at her sister. "You've got some nerve still using Jonathan's last name," she said.

Slate did not reply, but Reina could feel an electric charge pass between the sisters. At last Slate looked away, out the window, as if she wanted to flee.

"Could I . . . maybe . . . call you Amanda? No 'aunt'?" Reina asked. "You could be like a big sister or something." When Slate nodded her approval, Reina looked to her mother. "Is that okay?"

Mom shrugged. "Call her whatever you like. At least Amanda's *her* name."

"Emmy, please," Slate said. She closed her eyes. "The doctor says I need my rest."

"W-What's wrong with you?" Reina said, and waited patiently for Slate to drain her water glass before replying. Tuck was probably right; their aunt didn't look like the type to do drugs. She fidgeted at the thought of her brother. He must have totally drenched poor Brady; otherwise, they would surely be here by now. "You're going

48

to be okay, aren't you?" she asked her aunt.

Slate nodded again. "Exhaustion," she said. "Been working too hard. Too little sleep, too many gigs, too much travel, not to mention trying to write and rehearse in between. My voice, my body—everything kind of gave out at once."

Mom coughed at that, stood there shaking her head.

"How long are you going to have to stay here?" Reina asked. A strange fluttering sensation started in her stomach.

Slate shrugged. "Doctor says all I really need is a little chicken soup and bedrest." She glanced hopefully up at Mom, but Mom's expression was impassive.

"You could stay with us," Reina blurted, her heart beating fast. "Dad's mostly always gone on business." But it was obvious that there was no way Mom would want to share her room with Slate. "You could stay in my room. I've got a double bed, plenty of space."

"You're sweet. I'd really love to but—"

"I'm sure she'd be more comfortable in her penthouse over at the Sheraton, wouldn't you, Amanda?"

Reina glared at her mother. Mom was as bad as the Growl, putting the kibosh on anything that wasn't her idea.

A ruckus in the corridor announced the arrival of her brothers. Tucker bounded across the room, licking his fingers and punking up his hair. Brady hung back, peeking around Reina at the woman in the bed.

"Hey!" Tuck said, stopping short. "You're not Slate. What's going on here?"

"Yes she is," Reina said. "And I thought *you* were such a big fan."

Amanda's laughter turned into an exaggerated bout of coughing, which stopped as abruptly as it had begun. "He means my stage makeup," she said. "It's pretty outrageous, right?"

Tucker nodded and hoisted himself onto the foot of her bed. "You really *are* her? Jeez!" He drummed excitedly on the mattress. "This is so far out, I still can't believe it. Slate, *the* Slate, is my aunt. Amazing."

Mom let out a loud, disgusted sigh. "Tucker, please," she said. "I think it's time to go."

"No way. Me and Brady just got here. It's not fair."

"Please, Mama?" Brady said. "Just let us see her, okay?"

Reina added her own unspoken plea.

Mom sighed again, a decision in her silence.

"Lookee here. Razor's autograph." Tuck scooted closer to his aunt and reached for a pen on her night table. "Can I have yours, too?"

Mom caught his hand. "Writing on your jeans again, I see? I should let *you* spend thirty-five dollars a pair. Maybe *that* would make you take better care of them."

Reina tried to slide her hand over the black scrawl on her own jeans, but she'd have had to slouch even further and then Mom would notice for sure. Instead she nudged

Brady to stand in front of her, hiding the offense.

"Oh, Emmy," Amanda said, "they're just kids. Lighten up."

"Like *you* did?" Mom shot back. "You were so light, you floated away."

In the silence that followed, the tension grew like rising dough. Reina could hardly breathe. What had Amanda done that was so terrible? She seemed perfectly nice to Reina. Pretty, friendly, understanding—everything she'd always wanted in a sister. Mom was acting like a jealous witch.

Reina turned the possibility over in her mind as her brothers jabbered on. Maybe Mom *was* jealous. But who wouldn't be envious of a rich and famous sister? Slate had everything—money, fame, looks. And what did Mom have? A double major from Stanford that she'd never used, for starters. Plus two sons who drove her crazy, a daughter who wasn't even selected for the student council committee she'd created, a husband who was always on the road, and a little weekly column in *The Shopper*. Some exciting life. Maybe if Mom had become a big deal foreign correspondent in Latin America as she'd always dreamed, she would feel differently.

Reina glanced sideways at her mother, surprised to see her in this light. It was so much easier to cast her as the bad guy.

"Come on, boys," Mom was saying. "Time to go."

Tucker opened his mouth as if to protest, but Mom's

hard expression made him close it and peel himself off the bed. "When are you going to be better?" he asked.

"Soon, I hope. I've got a lot of commitments hanging over my head. And they say 'relax.' Ha! Easier said than done. Besides, me and hospitals don't exactly mix."

"You could stay with us," Brady offered. "I can help Mama make you breakfast. Cinnamon toast, just like when I'm sick. And I can bring it on a tray all by myself."

Amanda dabbed at her eyes with her bedsheet. "We'll see." She sniffed, looking up at Mom. God, she was practically begging her for an invitation. Reina squirmed.

"I'll be in touch," Mom said, taking Brady's hand. She nodded sharply at Tuck. "We're going. Now."

As Mom and her brothers swept past her, Reina bent over a bouquet of red roses on a table near Amanda's bed. She breathed in the memory of summer, wishing it, and she, could linger.

"Sweetie," Amanda said, "hand me a couple of those, will you?"

Reina pulled two long-stems from the vase. "Be careful," she said. "Thorns."

Amanda broke off both stems about four inches from the buds, then removed the remaining thorns. She nudged one rose behind her left ear and asked Reina to come closer. Then, smiling, she slipped the other behind Reina's right ear. "There!" she said, admiring her work. "You're my mirror image, do you know that?"

Reina's cheeks grew hot. All she could do was nod dumbly and bask in the glow of how strangely beautiful she felt at that moment. Bending forward, she kissed Amanda on the forehead. "Don't give up on Mom," she whispered. "I'm not. You'll see."

When Amanda said nothing, Reina traced her finger the length of her aunt's ebony hair, avoiding Amanda's eyes, then hurried off to catch up with the others.

The drive home was quiet agony. Even Tuck and Brady knew to keep their mouths shut. At each red light Mom glared across at Reina, then shook her head, apparently rejecting both angry words and the fact that her daughter had so disappointed her. As they bounced up the driveway, she said, "I want each one of you to go upstairs, put your pajamas on, get in bed, and start this day over again."

"You made us do that when we were *babies*," Tuck said.

"Well, you certainly acted like babies today." Mom parked the car and turned to Reina. "I can't believe you would do such a thing—humiliate me like that in front of my sister. You, who I can always count on. I'd expect it from the boys, but not you, Reina. Look at me. I'm sitting here shaking."

Reina swallowed hard. "I'm sorry. What else can I say?"

"I just don't understand why you'd treat me that way."

"What way?" Reina said.

"Siding with Amanda over me. You know nothing about her, absolutely nothing."

"What do you mean? I didn't side with anyone! And whose fault is it that I don't know my own aunt?" Reina blurted. Oh, God, she'd done it now. Disrespect. That was the worst offense. Cowering next to the door, she awaited her mother's tongue-lashing. She wouldn't get to call Nikki for a week. Maybe more.

"Go up to your rooms. Now!" Mom barked.

Reina shooed the boys into the house. When she looked back to see if Mom was coming, Mom was slumped over the steering wheel, her shoulders jiggling up and down. Reina hesitated in the doorway, wondering whether she should try to comfort her. But the sound of her father's voice leaving a message on the answering machine spurred her into the house.

She grabbed the kitchen phone off the wall. "Dad, wait! Don't hang up!" she cried, too late. An irritating buzz echoed in the black box as its red light began to blink. Reina quickly replayed the message: "Emily, it's me. Where is everybody? Call me at the Clarion in Port- land." And he left his number.

Dad would know what to do about Mom, she thought, and was just dialing his hotel when Tucker cranked up his tape deck. Raging noise seeped through the ceiling above her. She hung up the phone and pounded up the stairs, knocking on his door to no avail.

"Turn that down!" she yelled, entering without invitation. "I can't hear myself think."

Tucker was sitting on the edge of his bed, jerking his arms and head in time to the beat. "Slate," he hollered back. "Isn't she the greatest?"

Reina listened with new interest, but still heard nothing but unbridled rage.

"Whenever Mom ticks me off," Tuck said, "I slap in a little Slate and it calms me right down."

Weird, Reina thought. It was as though the music got angry *for* him. "Whatever," she said. "Just use your earphones so I can call Dad back."

Tuck obliged, for a change, and when she checked on Brady, he was looking at books on his bed. She redialed Dad's hotel, this time from her parents' room. Excitement bubbled up at the sound of his voice.

"How's my little queen?" he asked. "I can't believe you were up and out so early on a Saturday."

Reina explained about the alarm clock and about visiting Slate. "I don't know why Mom doesn't want her to come stay with us," she said. "It'd be fun, don't you think?"

"Well . . ." Dad cleared his throat. "I can see where it would be for you kids. But for your mom? I don't know."

"You two are always telling *us* to love each other no matter what. Why should I forgive Tuck for all the nasty things he does, when Mom won't even forgive Amanda?"

"I, uh, see your point," Dad said, after a long silence.

"Maybe it is time for those two to try patching things up."

"You think you could get her to change her mind?"

"I don't know. Is she still out there in the car?"

"I think so."

"Well," Dad said, "take the phone to her. I'll see what I can do."

Reina raced downstairs and into the garage with the cordless telephone. "Dad," she said, handing it into the car. "For you."

Mom accepted it, turning her back on Reina. Her voice was so low, all Reina could hear was an occasional hiccuping sound.

She backed away, not wanting to intrude. Dad obviously knew why Slate and Mom were on the outs. If he couldn't make her change her mind, Reina thought, nobody could.

She tried to imagine what it would be like, having a rock star staying at their house. Nikki was probably right; once the word got out, Sable was sure to appoint Reina to the planning committee. She bet Sable's eyes would turn even greener when she saw Razor's autograph on Reina's jeans. If only Dad could get through to Mom, Reina would be as good as voted in.

Pausing at the door, she looked over her shoulder at her mother. Tears glistened on Mom's cheeks, but from the hard set of her jaw, it looked like Dad had a lot more talking to do.

Monday morning before first period, Reina met Nikki, as planned, in the eighth-grade restroom. Her friend was glued to the mirror, applying another coat of blue mascara, edging out Carrie and a couple of other girls from the pom squad who were impatiently awaiting their turns.

"Hurry up, Stephenson," one urged. "What are you hoping for? Perfection?"

Nikki stuffed the wand back into its holder and smiled sweetly, as if the comment were a compliment instead of a cut. "It's all yours," she said, waving into the mirror at Reina.

She delayed a moment longer to fluff her hair, as Reina grabbed her arm, tugging her out of earshot of the others.

"*Nik*-ki, I thought you wanted to see his autograph,"

Reina chided in exasperation, holding up her thigh for inspection.

Nikki's eyes lit up, and she licked her lips. "You lucky dog! Razor's incredible, isn't he? But don't just show *me*," she said. "You've got to show *them*." She gestured toward the others, on the far side of the half wall.

"I will, I will. I just need you to help me get my courage up."

"Leave it to me." Nikki fussed with her clunky necklace. It looked as if it were made to go with her nubby, short-sleeved sweater. Why hadn't Reina worn something trendier? What would Carrie and the others think when they saw Reina wearing a crummy old sweatshirt with her Razor-autographed jeans? "Come on. Let's go tell 'em. Just remember our plan."

Nikki turned to go, but Reina grabbed her arm. "No, not yet. I'm too nervous."

"What's there to be nervous about? You've already met *him*. What I want to know is when do *I* get to?"

Reina shrugged. "I don't know. But Slate's being released today and—"

"And . . . and?" Nikki urged.

"And she'll be there when I get home." Reina grinned. "I don't guess you want to come over or anything, right?"

Nikki punched her arm playfully. A fresh cloud of hair spray boiled over from the main part of the bathroom;

Reina coughed. "Okay, it's now or never. If you don't hurry up and *do* something with my hair," she said, "it just might harden this way."

"Sure. Come on." Nikki nudged her back toward the others and took her comb. It was, of course, all part of their plan. While Nikki worked on Reina's hair, they'd both act nonchalant. Then, at just the right moment, when everyone was pushing around them, they'd spring Razor's autograph and set the bait. "Let me braid the side," Nikki suggested. "That'd be cute."

"Anything's better than this," Reina said, bending her knees. Alongside Nikki, she felt like a skyscraper. As Nikki's fingers flew, sectioning and plaiting her hair, Reina watched in her smidgeon of mirror. A couple of the girls nodded their approval.

"What'd you get on that Spanish test, Reina?" one of them asked.

Reina twitched her lips to one side, not wanting to answer.

"She got a hundred. As usual," the other said. "What do you want to bet?"

"I did all right."

"Yeah, what else is new?" Nikki teased, securing the braid with a rubber band. "You even got a solo in chorus. Sure wish your luck would rub off on me."

It wasn't luck. It was hard work. Reina squirmed, wishing someone would change the subject. It wasn't exactly

59

cool to be *too* smart. She nudged Nikki and pointed to Razor's autograph; it was time.

Nikki cleared her throat. "You guys want to see something cool? Check out Reina's jeans."

The girls drew closer, and Reina lifted her knee to the light. "Oh my God!" one squealed. "Razor Jamison! Look at that, Carrie! She's got his autograph!"

"Let *me* see that." Carrie studied the signature. "I can't believe it—*you,* at a Slate concert?"

Reina shook her head.

"Then how'd you get it?" Carrie said. "It's not real, right?"

"Oh, yes it is. Tell 'em, Reina." Nikki nudged her arm. "Go on. Tell 'em."

Reina felt her cheeks go hot. This was the big moment she and Nikki had so carefully rehearsed, and now she had stage fright. God.

"Rein-a." Nikki's hazel eyes telegraphed a much-needed dose of encouragement, but it didn't quite take. "All right, *I'll* tell 'em." She turned to the others. "Slate is Reina's aunt."

"Oh, really." Carrie's voice dripped with sarcasm.

"It's true," Reina managed. "I just found out this weekend."

"Come on, Williams, get real."

"I mean it. I got Razor's autograph when I visited her at the hospital."

The girls exchanged a questioning look. "If that's

true," one said, "why didn't you *know* she was your aunt? I mean, that *is* kind of weird."

Reina nodded, but was at a loss to explain, especially since she herself didn't understand why she hadn't known. Still, it was hardly *their* business that Mom and Amanda hadn't been speaking for years.

"It's a family thing," Nikki said, jumping in to fill the awkward silence. "You understand."

The girls nodded as if they did, and Reina grinned with relief. "She's being released today," she said. "And we're going to take care of her till she's better."

"Far out!"

"You mean it? You could get me her autograph?" Carrie said.

"She can do better than *that,*" Nikki said. "You can introduce them, right, Reina?"

"Well, I . . . uh . . . guess so. When she's up to it."

"She's staying at your house, huh, Reina?" Carrie finger combed a couple blond wisps onto her cheeks. "Wednesday's good for *me.*"

"Yeah, me, too."

A third girl nailed the others with a pointed look. "Carrie, I thought you said you've got a Comm-Comm meeting that day," she said. "Remember?"

"Oh, yeah." Carrie seemed chagrined to have forgotten. "Well, maybe another day."

"You could come over after you're done," Nikki said. "Or, better yet, why not meet at Reina's?"

"We really couldn't, unless Sable said . . . well, you know."

"Oh." Reina's disappointment dropped out of her mouth, uncensored.

Nikki said, "Maybe you could vote us onto the committee."

The girls looked at each other but said nothing. Absolutely nothing—as if they were *all* part of Comm-Comm. It wouldn't have killed Carrie, the only real member, to have at least offered a "maybe." Or even to have said that she'd talk to Sable. Instead she and the others just stood there, shifting their weight and eyeing the floor. Reina struggled to keep a hopeful smile in place as the choking sound of a flushing toilet reverberated throughout the green-tiled room. A fitting end to our hopes, she thought glumly.

"Well," Nikki continued, tugging on Reina's arm, "you guys think about it. With Reina's connections, I bet she could get Slate to stage a concert right here at Applewood."

Before the girls could respond, before Reina could protest, Nikki was dragging her out into the hall. "Stick with me, kid," she said. "We're gonna go far."

Reina wondered if the rest of the day crawled by because it was Monday and the teachers were still recovering from a big weekend or because she couldn't wait to get home. Maybe Nikki and the girls from the pom squad wanted to see Slate, the outrageous rock star, but all she wanted to see and get to know was Amanda, her new-found aunt. She almost wished she hadn't invited Nikki over. But after the way she'd bailed Reina out that morning in the restroom, Reina figured she owed her one.

Now, her house shimmered in humid silence as she and Nikki tossed their backpacks down in the mud room. She couldn't help being relieved that Tuck had gotten detention and wouldn't arrive until later. "Mom? I'm home," she called.

A muffled reply came from the basement room where Mom wrote her weekly column. What was she doing down *there*? Shouldn't she be upstairs with Amanda? Or had Mom changed her mind and decided not to invite her after all?

"Come on," Reina said, nudging Nikki toward the stairs.

In her room, she found Amanda unpacking a leather suitcase, wild clothes splayed all over Reina's bed. Amanda's dark hair, which fell to just below her waist, spun out like a cloak as she turned to greet them.

"I couldn't *wait* for you to get home," she said, her voice much stronger than on Saturday. "Look." She held up a sequined-and-baubled denim jacket. LAS VEGAS was spelled out on the back in tiny, blinking Christmas-tree lights. "It's for you."

Nikki's squeal made up for Reina's speechlessness. It was the most outrageously incredible jacket she'd ever seen in her life.

"You like it? Try it on."

Nikki gave her a little shove to unglue her feet. "Oh, Amanda, thank you!" She slipped her arms into the sleeves and paraded before the mirror. "It fits perfectly. How did you know?"

"ESP." Amanda laughed. "No, really. It was mine, but after I met you . . . well, let's just say I thought it'd look better on you."

Nikki ran her fingers lightly over the sequins. "Oooh, it's luscious," she said. "You're so lucky."

Reina grinned down at her, then gasped, suddenly remembering her manners. "Sorry," she said. "Amanda Slate, this is my best friend, Nikki Stephenson. Nikki, this is . . ." Giggles overcame her at the absurdity of continuing the introduction.

"Nice to meet you, Nikki," Amanda said. "Hmmm. Must be something funky around here for you, too." She fished through the clothes on her bed and at last held up a wide, snakeskin belt. "See what you think."

"Oh, I couldn't." But the glint in Nikki's eyes said otherwise.

"No, really. It's too tight for me. Don't know why I bought it in the first place."

"You're sure?" Amanda nodded, and Nikki buckled

the belt on. "It's beautiful! You're too much, you know that?"

"You're supposed to be resting," Reina said. "Why don't we hang up your stuff so you can get in bed?"

"It's all right. I can do it."

"No way. Reina's right." Nikki whisked the hanger from Amanda's hand. "Your fans need you. And how in the world are you going to finish your tour if you don't take it easy?"

Amanda nodded. "Right. My fans. Can't forget *them* now, can we?"

As Reina and Nikki hurried to clear the bed, Amanda rescued a pink satin nightgown from the pile and began undressing.

"Want us to leave?" Reina asked.

Amanda shook her head. "No time for modesty in my line of work," she said.

Nikki was oohing and aahing over each outfit that she hung in the closet. But Reina couldn't take her eyes off her aunt. Amanda was so slim, she could have passed for a boy were it not for her breasts. Silvery-white lines spidered the skin below, and on both sides of, her flat stomach. They looked just like the marks Mom got from gaining and losing weight a zillion times. Reina tried not to stare, and hoped her aunt hadn't noticed.

Amanda climbed into bed. "What's your mom up to anyway?"

Reina shrugged and leaned over to fluff up her pillows. "Probably working on her column. Hasn't she even come up to see if you need anything?"

"It's okay," Amanda said. "Don't be mad at her. She's busy, and this isn't exactly a planned visit."

Reina was sweltering in the LAS VEGAS jacket, but sudden outrage at Mom and loyalty to Amanda made her keep it on as she excused herself and raced downstairs.

She burst into her mother's study without knocking and stood there, glaring, her arms folded across her chest.

Mom kept typing. "And hello to you, too," she said, without looking up.

"I can't believe you're being like this." Reina sighed. "It's like I don't even know you anymore."

"What brought this on?" As Mom swiveled around in her chair, her eyes widened. "And where in God's name did you get that? It's Nikki's, right?"

Reina shook her head. "Amanda gave it to me. Isn't it great?"

Mom's face pinched up as if she'd just sucked a lemon. "You're serious?"

Reina nodded, but doubt stole in to erode her confidence. Though Mom could care less about how *she* dressed, she could always be counted on to select just the right pants and shirts for Reina.

"Honey, I really don't think it's 'you.' Besides, Mandy's going to need it for her little act, don't you think?"

"I don't know," Reina confessed. "I've never seen her videos."

"You haven't missed much," Mom muttered. As if she'd seen even one. "I'm sorry, honey, but I can't let you accept it. You'll just attract the wrong kind of attention at school, and anyway, it's too expensive."

"But—"

"No 'buts.' Please go give it back."

Whatever anger Reina had felt when she first came downstairs now multiplied tenfold.

"I won't!" she said. "It's mine! She gave it to me and I'm going to wear it. You can't stop me."

"Reina!" Mom flashed her a watch-your-mouth-young-lady look, but stopped short of sending her to her room.

The heavy metal music Reina so detested seemed to blare inside her. She stood taller, strangely empowered by it. Was this really the first time she'd dared to talk back to Mom?

"Go on," she said, goading her mother. "Why don't you send me to my room like you do Tuck? Is it because Amanda's there? Well, never mind. You needn't answer because I'm going. Gladly."

7

Reina slammed the door to her mother's study and raced upstairs. Phrases, bits of a poem perhaps, crashed around in her head over and over, like waves slamming against rock.

"What's with *you*?" Nikki said.

"Just a minute. Let me get this down." Reina retrieved her notebook from beneath the mattress and hurriedly scribbled the phrases:

> Don't get mad.
> (Don't let it get you down.)
> Don't get mad.
> (Don't think of what you've done.)
> Look at the monkeys
> up in the trees.
> Look at the plants

with their pretty leaves.
They don't have to do too much,
just anything they please.
And what about birds,
way up in the sky?
What do they do when
they don't want to fly?
You don't have to be the best
as long as you try.
Makes me stop and wonder why.

Boy, was this dumb. She wondered why she had even bothered to put it on paper. Looking up from the scribbled lines, she noticed Amanda reading over her shoulder.

"You write songs, too?" her aunt asked.

Reina blushed. "No, it's nothing, really. I just put down things that come to me. Usually when I'm mad."

"I know the feeling," Amanda said. "That's when I do some of my best stuff."

"Your songs are so cool," Nikki said. "You working on anything new? Maybe Reina and I could be your guinea pigs." She squinted at Reina and giggled. "Well, *I* could anyway."

Reina shot her a warning. That's all she needed—Nikki telling Amanda that Reina detested her music, nothing personal.

Amanda wrinkled her forehead, glancing from Nikki

to Reina. "What's that supposed to mean?"

Nikki cleared her throat. Reina held her breath, searching in vain for an explanation.

"Reina . . . ," Nikki said, "she's, well, . . . tone deaf."

"Really?" Amanda raised one eyebrow. "I thought your mom mentioned that you were in some special chorus at school."

She did? That meant that Mom and Amanda *had* spent some time together. Reina's feeling about her mother softened. Maybe Mom's on a deadline, she thought. If Amanda's not upset, why should I be?

Downstairs the front door slammed, and Reina was almost grateful to hear Tucker and Brady thundering up the stairs.

"Yippee! She's here! She's here!" Brady sang, bounding past Reina to kiss his aunt.

"Hey," Tucker said. He kicked off his smelly sneakers and left them inside the doorway.

"Go ahead," Reina said, her voice thick with sarcasm. "Make yourself at home."

Tucker ignored her gibe and turned to Slate. "Are you feeling good enough to sing a couple lines of 'Break Down the Walls' over the phone? I've got this friend E.J., see, and, well, he doesn't believe that you're staying here."

"Sweetie pie," she said, "if I tried to sing today, E.J. wouldn't believe you for sure."

"Oh." Tuck seemed momentarily subdued. But when he looked over at Reina, his eyes laughed like the devil.

"*I* know who could finish your tour for you," he said. "Reina! She's incredible. You ought to see how she sings into her true blue Secret in front of the mirror."

Reina gasped; her cheeks went hot. She grabbed Tuck by that wispy tail of hair he was trying to grow and twisted hard. Had he cried, she would have released him. But his hysterical laughter only angered her more. She thought of her threat to destroy his sugar-packet collection if he told E.J. what he'd seen. Well, she thought, he's done worse than that. He deserves what he gets.

Freeing him abruptly, she strode into his room, all business. Kicking clothes out of her way, she opened drawer after drawer in search of the stupid collection.

"You'll never find it," Tucker called from her bedroom. "Search all day if you want to."

"Nikki, come help me," Reina said.

Her friend appeared in the doorway and whistled at the mess. "Won't find anything in here," she said. "May as well give it up."

"No way. He's going to pay."

"He was just being funny," Nikki said. "Give the kid a break. If you hadn't overreacted, Slate never would have even believed him." She picked up a football-shaped pillow from the floor and tossed it playfully at Reina. "Do you *really* sing into your true blue Secret?"

Reina did not reply. Instead she locked Tucker's door, propping his desk chair under the knob as she'd seen in the movies. His platform bed was unmade as usual, and

71

she quickly rummaged through his bedding. Where could the kid have hidden that shoe box?

"Come on," Nikki said. "Let's go talk to Slate."

"You go if you want. I'm too embarrassed."

"Big deal. *Everybody* sings in front of the mirror."

Reina eyed her friend with surprise. "How do you know?"

"Simple." Nikki grinned. "I do it, too—with my hairbrush. And Mom said she even did it when she was a girl."

"You? And your *mom?*" Actually, Reina could picture Mrs. Stephenson doing such a thing. But her mind balked at the image of her own mother acting out rock and roll fantasies in front of the mirror. She suppressed a giggle.

"There now," Nikki said. "Feel better?"

"I guess." Reina looked back ruefully at Tucker's bed. "One packet. That's all I really wanted. Just one, so I could sprinkle it in his sheets and drive him crazy."

She stared at the platform, seeing it as if for the first time. Under the mattress. Of course. Why hadn't she thought of it before? Lifting one corner, she squinted into the dark space beneath the bed slats and spied his collection. From the shoebox she removed one packet, an easy-to-get one, from McDonald's. Then she sprinkled its contents in his bed and placed the package on his pillow.

"Mission accomplished?" Nikki asked.

"Definitely." Reina grinned. "What's say we go talk to

Amanda about Pom-Comm. Maybe she'll help us figure a way to get ourselves voted in."

But when they returned to Reina's room, Amanda was on the cordless telephone, deep in conversation. Brady had disappeared, and Tuck was fiddling with some perfume bottles on the dresser. "Couldn't find it, huh?" he said smugly. "I told you."

"Just go." Reina pointed the way. When Tuck left without taking his shoes, she tossed them into the hall and locked the door.

Amanda set down the phone. "You two hungry? The guys are bringing over a few pizzas. Pepperoni, extra cheese."

Nikki looked at her watch. "Shoot. Tonight's Mom's class. I've got to get home to baby-sit."

"Pain," Reina said. "Being the oldest is no fair. We ought to declare our freedom."

Nikki nodded glumly. "You can say that again."

Soon after she left, a limousine pulled up to the house. Razor Jamison and three other long-haired guys jumped out, each carrying a yellow box from Allegretti's, the most expensive pizza place in town. Nothing but the best for Slate, Reina thought as she opened the door.

"Hey, love," Razor said with a wink. "Las Vegas looks good on you."

Reina swallowed hard, her heart thumping in time to the blinking lights on her jacket. She stepped aside to let them enter. Too bad Sable Murphy didn't live on this street, she thought. Her eyes would have popped right out of her head at the sight of Razor Jamison, in the flesh. Not to mention the limousine. Once Sable recovered, she'd have called an emergency Pom-Comm meeting and voted Reina in for sure.

"Guys, this here's Slate's niece." Razor fumbled for her name.

"Reina," she supplied.

"Cool. That's 'queen' in Spanish, right?" said the only dark-haired guy.

She nodded, but didn't figure they would care to hear that Mom, the foreign-language whiz, had sold Dad on her unique name. Razor waded through the rest of the introductions. The other two blond guys were Warlock Hunt, the lead guitarist, and Duff Kohler, who played bass. Dark-haired Bobby Kale was on keyboards.

Reina mumbled, "Nice to meet you," which was a lie, really. Standing in the foyer, with their hair teased out past their shoulders and their jeans so tight that they concealed nothing, the band intimidated her, made her want to run downstairs to Mom's study. Only Razor's eyes held a softness that seduced her into staying.

"Well, love," he said, "lead the way."

Reina took to the stairs, wondering where Brady and Tucker could be. Not that she missed them. But it always helped to know ahead of time whether they might come popping in.

"Your band's here," she announced.

Amanda patted the mattress for Reina to sit down as the guys shuffled into the room. Bobby flipped open his box of pizza and soon everyone was sprawled on the floor, cheesy slices in hand.

"Let's blow some sounds," Warlock said, revealing a disgusting mouthful as he spoke. "Whatcha got?"

Reina bit her lip, felt her pulse quicken. Duff reached across the bed to rummage through the box of cassettes on her headboard. "Holy Christ! The Beach Boys!" He fell back on the floor, roaring with laughter. "What are you? A golden moldies freak?"

She rejected the truth, shaking her head.

"They're my sister's," Amanda said. "She's trying to torture me."

Reina flashed her aunt a grateful smile. "Yeah," she said, "she's so square you could play checkers on her." But the lie tied her stomach in knots, turning the cheese to rubber.

"More pizza?" Razor cracked open another box and passed it to Reina. She shook her head.

"Did you bring the tape?" Slate asked no one in particular.

Duff and Warlock paraded before her, accentuating their skintight jeans. "What you see is what you get, babe," one of them said. Reina had already forgotten which was which; they could have been twins.

Bobby patted himself down, but it was Razor who

75

found the tape in the pocket of his wild African-print shirt and flipped it over to Slate.

"Do you mind?" she asked Reina, and slipped the cassette into the player without awaiting a response. "It's stuff from our tour." She cranked up the volume. Heavy metal music exploded from the speakers.

Reina winced, then tried to hide her reactions. Razor patted her leg. "It gets better, love. Don't worry. Throw me a couple pencils, will you?"

Reina obliged, and soon Razor was drumming on the carpet, using her thigh as a high hat. The others picked at imaginary guitars, screaming out the lyrics at the top of their lungs. Amanda looked on in amusement at the makeshift instruments, lip synching after the music bridges.

Bobby tossed Reina an empty pizza box. "You do tambourine, babe. Knock yourself out," he said, demonstrating how to slap it against her hip.

Reina giggled and tried to worm out of it. But Bobby pulled her to her feet while the others cheered her on. "Go! Go! Go! Go!"

Reina looked to her aunt for reassurance. Amanda smiled and said, "Go for it."

Why not? Reina thought. It wasn't as if she had an audience. Not really. The guys seemed friendly enough. And this *was* still her room.

She stood up, shaking her head to loosen her inhibitions, and joined the jam session with her cardboard tambourine. Razor flashed her an Ultra-Brite smile that made her knees go weak. For all the racket the others made, for all their gyrations, Reina felt as if Slate's drummer were the only guy in the room.

Reina wasn't sure when the banging started. She only knew that all of a sudden Amanda snapped the tape player off and leaned back in bed, motioning the others to quiet down.

"Better see who's at the door." Amanda nodded at Reina.

It was probably Tucker. Or Brady, Reina figured. No big deal. "What do you want?" she said, a slight edge in her tone.

"I want you to open this door. Now." Mom's voice was cold enough to freeze blood.

Reina made a move to take her jacket off as Mom had told her earlier, then changed her mind. She glanced at Amanda and the others for courage as she opened the door.

Mom scanned the room, making no effort to hide her contempt for Amanda's visitors. "Excuse me," she said, "but this *is* my house."

"We weren't doing anything," Reina said. "Just having a little pizza and blowing a few sounds."

Mom's jaw dropped. "Blowing a few sounds? *Blowing* a few sounds?"

"Yeah," Reina said, aware of all the eyes trained on her. "What's wrong with that?"

"Emmy, please," Amanda said. "We were just having a little fun. No harm done, see?" Her gesture swept Reina's room.

Mom worked her jaw in silence for a long moment. "I think this is a mistake," she said at last, "you staying here, exposing the kids to this . . . this . . . lifestyle. Maybe you'd better make other arrangements. I'm sure you'll think of something."

8

"**M**o-om," Reina said. "You can't *do* that!" Anger burbled up from the pit of her stomach.

Mom trained her eyes on her sister and did not reply.

Razor cleared his throat and nodded to the other guys. "Why don't we go wait outside?" he said, collecting the empty pizza boxes.

Bobby, Duff, and Warlock gathered themselves up to their full height and leered down at Mom. She seemed not to notice. When the front door finally slammed behind them, she backed Reina into a corner, then whirled on her sister. "Do you ever think of anybody but yourself?" she said. "Do you?"

Amanda looked down, then drew the blankets up protectively.

"That's what I figured. Look. I'm trying to raise a family here, and I don't appreciate you waltzing in, filling their heads with all kinds of nonsense, trying to take over."

"I'm not," Amanda said.

Mom plucked at the sleeve of Reina's jacket. "Oh, no? What do you call *this?*"

"A gift. Since when is that against the law?"

"A couple-hundred-dollar one? Come on." Mom folded her arms across her chest. "Just what are you up to, Mandy?"

Amanda's violet eyes widened, all innocence.

Mom grunted. "You forget. *I* know you. The kids don't."

"So?"

"So every time I've let my guard down with you—every time I believe you've really changed—you've taken advantage of me. Over and over, the same old thing, and I'm tired of playing the fool."

"Oh, Emmy, please."

"I don't want that to happen to Reina," she said, "or to the boys, either."

Amanda sighed. "Calm down, Em, you're overreacting. As usual."

"Uh-uh. I don't think so." Mom was working her jaw the way Dad sometimes did when he was losing the checkbook balancing battle. "There's not an unselfish bone in your body. What do you want this time? My daughter? It's not enough that I don't get to see—"

"I want my *niece*," Amanda blurted. "And my nephews."

"What about *my* nephews?" Mom said. "Huh?"

Nephews? Reina thought. Slate didn't have any kids, did she?

"Let's not get into this," Amanda said. "Can't you accept that I'm sorry, and I—" She broke off, her voice catching with emotion. "I want my sister back, if it's not too late."

Mom bit her lip and looked away. Her chin was quivering. "I . . . I don't know," she said. Flicking a strand of hair off her forehead, she appeared to be fighting back tears.

"Emily, please? Can't we just start over?"

A squirmy silence filled the room. Sweat clung to Reina's bangs, trickled down between her breasts. Wriggling out of the jacket, she hoped Amanda didn't think she was taking Mom's side. How could she? She didn't even understand what Mom's side was. But even if her mother was jealous, as Reina had figured before, that was no reason to take it out on Amanda.

"Emily, please?" Amanda persisted, her voice small. "Just give me another chance."

"Come on, Mom. You're always telling me to forgive Tuck, remember?" Reina patted her mother's hand. "What if we say the guys won't come over anymore? Okay, Amanda?"

"I promise," her aunt replied, holding up two fingers.

Mom rolled her eyes and heaved a great sigh. She looked as if she were resigning herself to going with Reina on the Crazy Dipper ride at the junior fair. At last she crossed to the bed and, with a sour little chuckle, lifted Amanda's ring finger. "You always were a lousy Girl Scout, weren't you?" she said, shaking her head. "Oh, all right. You can stay. But no more loud parties. And no expensive presents without my permission. Agreed?"

Amanda nodded. Reina rushed forward to embrace her aunt, but stopped short when she saw the unmistakable wince of pain in her mother's eyes.

"Thanks, Mom." She managed to give her mom a quick, awkward hug. "Well . . ." She backed toward the door, feeling strangely uncomfortable in her own room. "Guess I'll, I don't know, go out and tell the guys."

Reina had no chance to talk to Amanda again until after she went to bed. Though it was past ten, Tucker was still down in the kitchen, being coached through his math homework by Mom.

"If I can get all *my* homework done on time," Reina said into the darkness, "I don't see why *he* can't."

Amanda grunted. "I was the same way when I was a kid. Always trying to stay up later than Emmy, getting Mama to spend time alone with me."

She rolled onto her side, and Reina could feel her aunt's breath, minty cool upon her cheek. "If he's anything like me, that's all he's after. Attention, with a capital A."

"I suppose. But it really bugs me how he gets whatever he wants by being a pain."

"If it works," Amanda said, "why fix it?"

"Wish *I* could find something that worked for me." Reina fell silent, wondering whether she should talk to Amanda about Pom-Comm, about how important it was to be accepted by Sable and the others.

"You'll find something, sweetie pie. All you need is yourself and today. And you've got both of those, right?"

"I don't see how that'll get me on the community action committee," Reina said.

"Community action, huh? Is it important to you?"

"It's a lot more than the name says." Reina ran her fingers lightly over the sheet. "It's like, the kids on it—the chairman—you're nobody till they say you are," she said. "Nikki thinks you could help us, but—" She broke off, unable to explain her doubts. She didn't want to be "in" just because she had a famous aunt, did she?

"But you don't want to use me, right?" Amanda chuckled. "Well, use away, sweetie. I'll be glad to do whatever I can."

Reina reached over to hug her aunt, tangling her fingers in Amanda's long hair. "You're the greatest," she whispered.

"So are you," Amanda whispered back.

Reina lay in the darkness for the longest time, trying

not to squirm with excitement over Amanda's willingness to help. At last she heard Tucker banging around in the bathroom, making a big production of running the water, flushing the toilet, and slamming the lid. "See, Reina?" he called. "Can't say I never put it down."

Reina flipped the sheets aside, her heart pounding. The little brat had read her journal. "I'm going to kill him," she said.

"Boys." Amanda sighed. "Just . . . ignore . . ." Her voice seemed to drift out of her.

"I'll be right back."

The hall light snapped off. Tucker's dark silhouette scurried past, and Reina tiptoed after him. She heard the rustling of his covers, then a muttered curse. "Hey," he said, "what the—"

Reina clapped her hand over her mouth to contain a giggle. The sugar! She'd almost forgotten. Hurrying back to bed, she rolled toward Amanda and pretended to sleep, all the while gathering gleeful satisfaction from Tucker's discomfort.

"I finally got him," she whispered to her aunt.

"Mmmm-hmmm."

"Amanda? Remember what Mom said today? About her having nephews?"

"Mmmm-hmmm."

"What was she talking about?" When Amanda did not respond, Reina nudged her lightly.

"Ivan," she murmured. "Jeremy." Amanda's little

chewing noises made Reina suspect that her aunt was talking in her sleep.

She thought about the silvery-white marks on her aunt's stomach. Maybe they were stretch marks from having babies, not from gaining weight. "Amanda, pssst! Wake up. Tell me. Ivan and Jeremy—are they your kids?"

Amanda snored softly in reply, and though Reina stared hard at her through the darkness, she did not awaken.

The next day Reina was waiting for Nikki in the hot-lunch line when Sable Murphy squeezed in front of her. "Cuts?" she said, grinning that dimpled smile that no one ever said no to. "You mind?"

Reina shook her head. Whatever Sable Murphy wanted, Sable Murphy got.

"You remember Comm-Comm, my new student council committee, right?" Sable said, her voice weaving confidential webs around them both. "Well, we've got this little problem, and I thought maybe you could help us out."

Reina's shrug belied the sudden pounding in her chest. Nikki was right; Sable was going for the bait as planned.

She drew so close, Reina could smell her herbal shampoo. "We're supposed to have a recommendation to take to student council on Friday. You know, about a service project thingie. But, well, we haven't come up with a plan yet. And if we don't do something to justify our existence, Mr. J.'s going to be all over us, you know?"

"So?" Reina said.

"So we've got to come up with an idea. Quick."

"Why don't you go with a fundraiser?"

"Yes, but what kind?" Sable asked. "Any ideas?"

"You act like I'm a member." As she waited for Sable's reply, Reina's palms began to sweat around the change she was holding.

"That *could* be arranged," Sable said, "for the right idea."

Reina caught Nikki waving at her from the salad line on the other side of the cafeteria and flashed her an A-OK sign behind Sable's shoulder. "W-What about Nikki?" she asked.

"What about her?"

"Can't you vote *her* in, too?"

Sable tossed her copper-colored hair over her shoulder. "Look, Nikki's got to earn her own way, same as you. Besides, she's kind of phony, don't you think?"

"Phony?" The word stuck in Reina's throat.

"You know, the way she dresses. JoNelle said she saw her last week coming out of Goodwill with a whole bagload of stuff."

"What's wrong with—"

"Like, oh-my-god, Reina. Really." Sable scalded her with a look. "You want in, or you wanna stand here, talking about—how shall I put this?—our friendly bag lady?"

Reina winced. "Are you saying there's no chance you'd appoint Nikki?"

"*Moi?* Oh come now. I never say never." Sable let loose a little harpsichord laugh. "So. Do you have an idea for us or not? I was thinking maybe your aunt could help."

"My aunt? How do you mean?"

"You know. Maybe she could do a concert or something."

"A *benefit.* Yeah. Like for the homeless or something. Sure! Soon as she's better, I bet she'd do it. For *me* she would, definitely."

"Great!" Sable said. "I knew we could count on you."

"But . . ." Reina licked her lips and began again. "What I mean is—"

"Well, spit it out, Williams. We don't have all day."

Reina glanced at Nikki. "When will I know if I'm —you know—*in?*"

"First you deliver Slate, then we'll poll the committee."

Reina mustered a confidence she didn't quite feel. "I'd try a lot harder with my aunt if I were a member."

"I guess you would," Sable said. "Well, I'll do my best."

Reina nodded, jacking up the corners of her mouth.

"It's a deal then?" Sable patted her arm. "Keep me posted, okay?"

"You'll be the first to know," Reina said, but Sable was already moving ahead in line, cutting in front of some guy on the football team.

Nikki left the salad line and hurried over, her fringed scarf flapping like a broken wing. "Well? What'd she say? What'd *you* say? Are we in or what?"

Reina sighed and rubbed her forehead. "Not yet."

"What's wrong? What? You can tell me."

"It's . . . nothing," Reina said, but the evasion made her empty stomach feel queasy. She had never lied to Nikki before. Ever. But then she had never felt she had to protect her friend, either.

"Nothing. Right." Nikki fidgeted with her scarf clip, avoiding Reina's eyes. "It's about me, isn't it?"

Reina shook her head. "Why does everything have to be about you?" she snapped.

Nikki flinched as if she'd just been struck. She blinked back tears, smudging her mascara. "Is that what you think, Reina?"

Reina wished desperately that she could take it all back. "I-I didn't mean it. Really." She fished through her purse for a tissue. "Here," she said. "I guess I was mad at Sable, and I took it out on you."

"You're sure?" Nikki dabbed at her eyes but only made things worse.

"Let me," Reina said. The lunch line shuffled forward as she blotted blue smears off Nikki's cheeks.

At last Nikki asked why Reina was so upset.

"She's blackmailing me," Reina said, not untruthfully. "I've got to come across with a benefit concert so Pom-Comm can justify its existence. And then they'll vote me . . . us . . . in." She checked Nikki's reaction to see if she'd noticed Reina's change in wording, but Nikki was already brainstorming plans for the benefit.

"See? I told you it would work. Should it be for the homeless or what? How about for leukemia research or juvenile diabetes? How are we going to decide? I mean it, Rein, there're so many good causes, aren't there?"

Reina nodded, ashamed that she could stand there and hide the truth from her best friend. She was sure Sable was just jealous of Nikki's looks and flair with clothes. It took real talent to be able to go through someone's rejects and put together a trendy outfit that anyone else would pay through the nose for at Levandeau's. Reina bet that, deep down, Sable was afraid that once Jamey and the others got to know Nikki, they'd like her better than Sable.

Once I'm voted in, she thought, I'll make them all see what a great person Nikki is. But first, I have to get voted in.

"Reina?"

"Hmmm?"

Nikki handed her a tray. "I can feel it," she said. "We're almost in. Think so?"

Reina tried to cough away the lump in her throat. "Yeah, Nikki," she said. "We're almost in."

9

As Reina set the supper table, she wondered when Amanda would be off the phone. Her aunt had been on it nonstop—long distance, too, judging by a few snips of overheard conversation—ever since Reina had gotten home from school, and she was dying to ask about the benefit concert. Surely her aunt would agree to do it. Hadn't she already said "Use away, sweetie. I'll be glad to do whatever I can"?

Anyway, since Amanda *had* collapsed in the middle of her show last weekend, didn't she practically owe the community another chance to see her? The middle-school gym would be too small, of course. But maybe they could stage it outside on the football field, or, better yet, at Elver Park. Maybe the deejays at Z104 would even help promote it on the air.

"Reina," Mom said, "you seem a billion miles away."

90

"I was just thinking." She caught Mom staring at the haphazard way she'd strewn the napkins and silverware about and hurried to straighten the place settings. "There's this student council committee I want to be on—the community action committee?"

Mom nodded, and Reina hurried on. "Anyway, I've got a chance to be appointed. A chance to be in with all the popular kids. Isn't that great?"

"Since when aren't you popular?"

Reina shifted her weight and stared at the floor, chiding herself for having even broached the subject with her mother. Maybe Tuck was right; Mom *was* a square. What she understood about popularity probably wouldn't fill an eye-dropper. Could it be that back in the sixties, when Mom was in high school, Mom was just as nerdy as she seemed in her yearbook picture? The possibility made Reina squirm; she'd been so accustomed to thinking of her mother as basically acceptable.

"I guess I'm *kind of* popular," she admitted at last. "It's just that I wouldn't mind getting invited to a few parties now and then—or having a hunk for a boyfriend."

"Mmmm." Mom nodded knowingly.

"Look, *you* know Amanda. Do you think she'd do a benefit concert at our school?"

"She might," Mom said, "if she's the one who benefits."

"Mo-om."

"I'm sorry. That wasn't nice." Mom set a bowl of salad

and a loaf of steaming garlic bread on the table, then called Tucker and Brady for dinner. She turned to Reina. "Let's just say I'd be very surprised. But why don't you ask her? See for yourself how she is. Mandy's good at many things. But putting others' needs ahead of her own has never been one of them."

"You're talking about Ivan and Jeremy, aren't you?"

Mom eyed her sharply. "So you know about your cousins, huh? I'm surprised Amanda told you."

"She didn't exactly," Reina said. "I kind of figured it out. Why the big secret?"

Mom shrugged. "No secret, really. It's just that she walked out on them and their dad five years ago and hasn't looked back. Had to 'go for it,' she said, before it was too late." Mom dried her hands on her apron, avoiding Reina's eyes. "It hurts knowing I have nephews out there that I'll never see or get to know."

"What's stopping you?"

Mom looked shocked. "Well, I . . . I don't even know where they are, for one thing. Besides, it'd be too . . . awkward."

"Why awkward?"

"What would I say to them? About Mandy, I mean. What would I say to their father? They all must feel so angry and abandoned."

"Jeez, Mom," Reina said. "You act like *you* left them, not Amanda."

Mom avoided Reina's eyes and began nervously

straightening clutter on the countertop. "We weren't raised to be irresponsible like that," she said at last. "I'm ashamed for her." She narrowed her pale blue eyes at Reina. "How would *you* feel if I up and moved to Argentina to report the news?"

"Bad," Reina said, trying unsuccessfully to imagine something so unthinkable. "But you'd never do that, would you?"

Mom's twisted smile made Reina shiver. "There are days when I sure fantasize about it," she said. "You think it's easy, raising three kids with a husband who's always on the road? Don't get me wrong. I love you. And your father. But . . . I don't know. I can't help thinking there's supposed to be more . . . more passion in life."

"Like what Amanda's got?"

"Maybe so. Maybe I do envy her that. But you don't go leaving your kids to find it. It's just not right."

Reina slipped her arm around her mother's shoulder. "Lucky for us you feel that way," she said.

Squirming out of the compliment, Mom glanced around self-consciously as if the papered walls had ears. "Those boys! You need to call them a million times before they come."

"I'll get them," Reina offered. "You sit down and relax."

"Thanks, honey. Have I ever told you how much I appreciate you?"

"Yes," Reina said, but she wondered why Mom only

seemed to appreciate her when she was helping out around the house. Wasn't there more about her to love than that? Nudging the thought aside, she went to fetch her brothers.

Brady thumped down the stairs on his bottom, his head jiggling as if it were spring-mounted. Tucker lagged behind, to make sure Amanda was coming, too.

"What're we having?" Brady said.

"Spaghetti." Mom ladled a small clump onto his plate.

"Yuck! I hate sugetti. It tastes like worms."

"Since when don't you like worms?" Mom said. "Come on and sit down now. Stop all this nonsense."

Brady took his seat grudgingly, glowering at his food. "And I'm not eating salad, either," he said. "Just the crunchies."

Mom sighed. "Fine. Suit yourself."

Reina took her place beside Mom. Moments later Tucker strolled in, hand-in-hand with Amanda. She was wearing an exotic blue caftan with an embroidered design of silver curlicues across the chest and down both sleeves.

"You're looking much stronger," Mom said, indicating the chair beside Brady's. "When do you see the doctor again?"

"The end of the week. Mind if I turn the TV on? My agent says our latest video may top the charts."

Without waiting for Mom's reply, Tucker leaped from his chair to swivel the television around from the adjoining family room. "Which one? 'Break Down the Walls' or 'Pandora's Box'?"

"We'll just have to see now, won't we?" Amanda's eyes glowed with anticipation.

The set crackled to life, and Tucker quickly changed it to MTV.

"We're not 'posed to watch TV while we're eating," Brady remarked. "Mama said."

"Who's eating, Brady?" Tuck shot back. "Not you, that's for sure."

"All right, all right." Mom sighed in resignation. "Leave it on."

"Who knows, Em?" Amanda teased. "You might even like it."

The countdown ticked from five to four to three to two. "And in the number one slot this week," Veejay Tommy Peyser announced, "up from number three, is Slate with 'Break Down the Walls'!"

Beneath the table, Reina clapped her hands. Tucker whooped and turned up the volume, while Brady stole over to sit on Mom's lap. White-lettered credits flashed in the lower left of the screen as the camera panned along walls. Some were famous, like the Great Wall of China and the Berlin Wall. Others anonymous—graffiti-covered red brick, perhaps from some inner-city playground.

The drums began like an echoing heartbeat, with

95

Razor's image superimposed over the walls. Then, in a flash of white light, a distant scream—part human, part guitar—accompanied a new image of tears and blood washing together across the screen. The camera zoomed in on a black-clad figure standing defiantly atop a wall, belting out the lyrics.

At first Reina thought it was Bobby because of the dark hair that stood on end as if it were electrified. But the singer's features—what she could see anyway, beneath the blue painted butterfly and gold glitter—were too feminine to belong to the keyboard player. "Amanda, is that really you?" she asked, transfixed by the singer's emotion as much as by her outrageous makeup.

"That's me, all right." She laughed softly. At herself, Reina thought, not at me.

"I like the lyrics," Mom said. "Powerful stuff. Did you write it?"

"Of course I did." Amanda's response shot back like a Ping-Pong ball. "I write all our songs."

Mom's eyes widened in surprise. "Excuse me for asking," she said. "I never took you for a poet is all. You don't have to get bent out of shape."

"I'm not." Amanda turned her attention back to the TV, and Reina followed suit.

The credits flashed again at the end of the video. The veejay broke in with an MTV Newsbreak. "This just in from our correspondent in Chicago," he said. "Our girl

Slate is going to need a pretty speedy recovery to make her court date on October—"

Amanda jumped up and snapped off the TV.

"Hey," Tuck said. "I wanted to hear that. Turn it back on." He lunged for the set, but Amanda intercepted him.

"It's just business stuff," she said. "Nothing important. We saw the video. That's what mattered."

Mom eyed her questioningly but said nothing as she shooed Brady back to his seat and passed her sister the spaghetti.

Why would Amanda be due in court? Reina wondered. Maybe it had something to do with divorce. Or maybe . . . Her pulse raced with the possibility. "You're trying to get your kids back, right?" she said.

"My kids?" Amanda blinked at her, uncomprehending.

"Remember Ivan and Jeremy?" Reina heard the irritation in her voice but made no attempt to conceal it. Leaving them was bad enough, but forgetting them?

"Of course." Amanda recovered her composure. "I didn't know Emily had mentioned them."

"She didn't," Reina said. "You did last night. In your sleep."

"Oh. Well." She looked down at her hands as Tucker and Brady stared. "The court thing isn't about them. They live with their father and . . . well, I'm sure they're happier that way."

"I miss *my* daddy," Brady said.

"Of course you do." Mom ruffled his hair. "Daddy will be home in a few more weeks, as soon as his training seminars are over. You know that. Now eat your dinner, okay?"

Brady slurped up one long strand of spaghetti. The tail dotted his nose with sauce. "Feed me, Amanda," he said, handing her the next forkful.

She reached out to block it, but bumped his hand instead, spilling meat sauce and pasta on her caftan. "Oh, look what you've done!" she wailed, recoiling. "I've never known a little boy yet who could eat over his plate!"

Reina gasped. "It wasn't *his* fault," she blurted.

Amanda seemed to shrink at the rebuff. "Of course it wasn't. You're absolutely right. You see? I have no patience for this mothering stuff. Always blaming and saying the wrong things." She turned to her sister. "You may not think so, Emmy, but Ivan and Jeremy *are* better off with Jonathan. I have to believe that."

"Of course you do," Mom said, almost sarcastically. She filled Reina's milk glass and cleared her throat. "Wasn't there something you wanted to ask Amanda?"

"Oh yeah. The benefit." She toyed with her spaghetti, pushing it around the plate with her fork. She hadn't envisioned having to talk to Amanda about Sable in front of her mother. Mom would only say that Reina needed friends like Sable Murphy like she needed a hole in her head, and Reina didn't need Mom on her back about

Sable right now. She already felt guilty enough about the way things were with her and Nikki.

"What benefit, sweetie?" Amanda said.

"Remember those friends I told you about? The ones at school?"

"The—"

"Yes, you've got it." Reina inclined her head toward Mom, hoping Amanda would catch her meaning. "Well, they asked me to help them with a service project, and I came up with the idea of a benefit concert. What do you think?"

"A benefit for what?" Amanda said.

"Whatever you want."

"Oh, *I* get it." Amanda laughed. "I'm doing the concert, right?"

"Only after you're all better, and only if you want to. Pretty please?"

"And if I say yes, you'll live happily ever after, right?"

Reina grinned. "Something like that."

Amanda managed a last bite of spaghetti, then pushed her plate aside. "I should think you'd want to be accepted for who *you* are, Reina. Not for who you're related to."

"B-But . . ." Reina turned to her mother, certain Mom must have spoken her thoughts to Amanda.

Mom just shrugged. "I didn't say a word. But I'm glad Mandy and I can agree on one thing at least."

"Mom! Amanda!" Reina glowered at them both.

"Now, now," her aunt said. "I didn't say I wouldn't do it."

"You will then?" Reina's pulse quickened.

"On one condition."

"Name it," Reina said. "Anything."

"I want you to come out of the closet, Reina, and sing with us."

Reina's mouth went dry. Sing with Slate? Was she crazy? If the music didn't kill her, she thought, a case of stage fright surely would.

Amanda turned to Mom. "Please, Emmy. You yourself told me how talented she is, what a great voice she's got. It'd be fun. The chance of a lifetime."

Oh, please, Mom. Be my excuse. Get me out of this. Reina watched her mother's face for a frown, a scowl, some sign of a no. Focusing her thoughts, she beamed them toward her wonderful, square mother and waited.

"Come on, Mom," Tucker said, his mouth full. "Let her do it. Don't be a poop."

"Well . . . I don't know. Let me think about it."

Think? What's there to think about? Reina almost screamed. Be your old Beach-Boys-lovin' self. Say no! Reina could hardly breathe.

Mom's jaw seemed to be moving in slow motion. At last her decision growled out like a microcassette played at half speed: "Su-u-r-r-e. W-h-h-y n-o-o-t-t?"

100

10

Her homework finished, Reina grabbed the cordless phone, locked herself in the bathroom, and called Nikki. "What am I going to do?" she said. "Maybe I should just tell Amanda I can't, that I've got a weak heart or something, that it couldn't take all that excitement."

"Very funny. You wouldn't dare."

"I know," Reina said miserably. "But I'm not kidding. I swear I'll have a heart attack if I have to get up there and sing that . . . that . . . *music* in front of everyone."

"No you won't. Don't you see? Sable and those guys, they'd kill to be in your shoes. What we've got to do is create a whole new image for you. A stage presence."

"Right," Reina said. How could Nikki get so excited about impending disaster?

"I'm serious. We'll change your hair, for real this time. Put on some wild makeup. Get you an awesome outfit."

She paused, and Reina could almost hear Nikki's imagination crackling through the phone. "A stage name, that's what you need. Slate and Reina sounds dumb, right? But how about . . . let me think. Wait, wait, something's coming to me."

"Nikki, forget it. There's no way I'm going to stand up there next to Amanda and look like anything but a jerky eighth grader, and you know it."

"Rain! How does that sound? 'Ladies and gentlemen, I give you Slate and Rain.' Is that great or what?"

Reina laughed. "Okay, okay. I admit, it does sound pretty good. But—"

"But nothing," Nikki said. "I'm sure Amanda will help you find the right look, and all *you've* got to do is practice with Razor every day until the concert. Not bad, I'd say."

"Dream on." Reina rehung the towels that Brady and Tuck had slopped over the bar after their showers. "Amanda's got a *tape* I'm supposed to practice with."

"Oh. Look, I have to go," Nikki said. Reina could hear the twins squabbling in the background. "See you tomorrow at school, *Rain*. Oh, wait! I almost forgot to tell you. I bought a new issue of *Metal Mania,* and it's supposed to have a whole big write-up on Slate. I'll bring it, okay?"

"Sure."

"What do you bet I won't be able to sleep?" Nikki said. "It's almost Wednesday. And you know what *that* means."

"What?" Reina asked.

"Pom-Comm meets, that's what."

"Oh. Yeah."

"Cheer up," Nikki said. "No way they'd keep us out, now that we've got the concert nailed down." The "we" stabbed at Reina's conscience. But how could she tell her best friend that half a dream come true was better than none—at least for now?

Reina lay in bed listening to Amanda's slow, even breathing. She tried to picture herself on stage, performing for Slate's fans. Maybe Nikki was right about becoming a whole new person; it would free her to behave in strange and wild ways. But what about the music itself? Slate's melodies and lyrics weren't so bad, but those amplified, screaming guitars were another matter. It would definitely *not* be cool to shrivel up her face and cover her ears right there on stage.

Grinning at the image, she wondered whether ear plugs would help and decided—what the heck!—they were worth a try. Because there was no turning back now. She was too close to "happily ever after."

The next morning, in English, Nikki passed her a note that said, "I've got a dentist appointment during lunch, so meet me after school at Sentry. I've got a *T-rrific* idea about your hair." "T-rrific" was written in fatsausage like letters and underlined three times.

Reina wasn't sure whether the knots in her stomach all day were from excitement or fear. What did Nikki have in mind? Sure, *her* hair always looked great (even when she'd cut it herself). But who could go wrong with thick, wavy, cooperative hair like *she* had?

After school Reina crossed at the light and hurried the extra block to the neighborhood supermarket. With Indian summer pressing heavily about her, she longed to be inside the air-conditioned store. But a sign on the automatic door stopped her cold: No school-aged children admitted without a parent or a parent's note before 4 P.M.

Great. Now what were they going to do? When Nikki finally rushed across the parking lot, breathless and apologetic, Reina blurted out the store's posted rule.

Nikki grinned mysteriously. "Don't worry," she said. "Stick with me, kid. We're gonna go far."

"You always say that. But where's the proof?"

Nikki pulled a note from her backpack. "Voilà!"

Reina squinted at the cramped handwriting. "Your mom wants you to buy some hair dye? Are you kidding?"

Nikki rolled her eyes, grabbed Reina's arm, and dragged her into the store. She handed the note to the cashier, who indicated the proper aisle.

"See?" Nikki giggled. "I think of everything. I told you to stick with me." She ran her finger along the shelves of boxed hair-coloring kits. "Which brand do you want?"

"This is for *me*? No way, Nikki," Reina said. "You're crazy."

Nikki blew out a long, exasperated breath. "I thought we agreed to make you over. What are we *doing* here, then? I could be home cleaning my room. Or better yet, baby-sitting. No, really. I'm just kidding. Don't you trust me?"

Reina slouched, rubbing her forehead. "Look, it's not that. It's just, well, don't you think I'd look kind of sleazy as a bleached blonde?"

"Blonde?" Nikki clapped her hand over her mouth to contain her laughter. "Who said anything about blonde? You're going slate black. Get it?"

Reina groaned. "You're as bad as Tuck." She fingered a sweaty length of hair, imagined it as shiny and as silky as her aunt's. "You sure you know how to do this?" she said. "It won't turn orange or anything?"

"Not if we buy the good stuff. L'Oreal, what do you think?"

Reina shrugged. It looked okay on the TV commercial models. But what did she know?

"How about Preference?" Nikki took the box off the shelf and handed it to Reina.

"It says 'permanent hair coloring'," Reina said. "What if I don't like it?"

"Here, try this." Nikki handed her another product, Avantage in "natural black." "Washes out after six shampoos."

"All right," Reina said, still unconvinced. "But if it wrecks my hair, you owe me a professional makeover."

"Deal."

After paying for the hair dye, they caught the city bus

in front of the market and got off at Canterbury. "I think we'd better do this quick, before I lose my nerve," Reina said.

"Fine with me."

The house was locked, and Reina used her key. Mom's note asked her to watch the boys; she and Amanda had gone to the doctor's. Nothing serious; he'd had a cancellation.

"Boy, are *we* in luck," Reina said, remembering that Brady had nursery school and Tuck stayed after school on Wednesdays to play floor hockey. "By the time everyone gets home, the deed will be done-da-done-done." She sang out the last word like a death knell.

Nikki rolled her eyes at Reina's attempted humor. "We'd better hurry up. We've only got a half hour before your brothers get home."

While Nikki read the directions aloud from the bathroom, Reina changed into an old T-shirt. Her heart was pounding as she sat down on the commode. This was no big deal. A different look, that's all. Why was she blowing it all out of proportion?

Nikki snipped the cap off the tube and put on the clear plastic gloves. Then she squeezed the dye throughout Reina's dry hair. "Hand me that shower-cap thing," she said, and stuffed Reina's hair into the plastic bag. "Now you've got to leave it for thirty minutes."

"Great. What if Tucker sees me?"

"He won't." Nikki pulled her *Metal Mania* magazine

from her backpack and handed it to Reina. "Lock the door and stay put. I'll go watch for the boys."

Reina glanced nervously at her watch. "You won't forget to take this off, will you?"

"No way. Just relax."

Reina locked the door and sat down to read the magazine. Finding the photo feature about Slate on page twenty, she quickly scanned the text. There at the bottom was a small boxed bulletin, apparently inserted at the last moment:

"Amanda Slate is due in federal court in Chicago on October 22 to answer plagiarism charges filed by songwriter Joe-D Summers over the lyrics to Slate's chart-topping 'Break Down the Walls.' Summers alleges in his complaint that he submitted a tape recording of his song 'Bust Down the Walls' to Slate last year along with a cover letter asking if she would be interested in purchasing the rights and recording it. Slate reportedly returned the tape with a polite rejection, but, according to Summers, recorded the song anyway as if it were her own. Slate could not be reached for comment."

Reina's pulse quickened. The newsprint blurred and she set the magazine aside. Amanda couldn't have stolen that song. She herself said that she did all her own writing. Besides, a person that famous wouldn't dare do anything so stupid, would she? That Summers guy must just be trying to get rich quick.

After a while, she could hear Brady and Tucker arguing

about something downstairs, their voices echoing off the walls. Some dispute about baseball cards, as if stupid pieces of cardboard were worth fighting about. Nikki stepped in to referee, and soon the TV was blaring from the family room.

Reina looked at her watch, wondering why Nikki hadn't returned to rinse off the dye. She cracked the door, listening for her friend's footsteps on the stairs. The doorbell rang. Somebody looking for Tucker probably. But Nikki still did not return.

Reina stared at herself in the mirror. What had she done? Just because black hair looked great on Amanda, it didn't mean it'd look good on her. What was next? Violet contacts? A nose job? Where *was* Nikki anyway?

Swathing her head in a towel in case Tuck came out of the family room, she hurried downstairs. "Nikki?" she called. "I thought you said—" She swallowed her words as she rounded the corner and came face to face with Sable Murphy. "W-What are *you* doing here?" she asked, touching her turban self-consciously. At least it looked as if she'd only been washing her hair.

"We just had our meeting," Sable said. "Thought you'd want to hear what we decided." She strolled into the living room. "Pastels," she said, dismissing the decor with a glance. "Ours is champagne and gold."

Reina said nothing. What was wrong with their living room? And who, besides Mom, even cared what color it was?

"Ours is teal and peach," Nikki said. "Yummy. I helped with all the decorating myself. Fabrics, drapes, even the new carpet. You ought to see it, Sable."

Sable fingered a blown-glass swan and did not reply. Nikki bit her lower lip, her eyes downcast.

"So, are we going with the concert or what?" Reina said.

Sable ignored the question. "Where's Slate? I thought you said I could get her autograph."

"At the doctor's," Reina said with an apologetic shrug. "A checkup. She'll be back later."

"Oh. Well." Sable pouted. "Hold out your hand, then." She pressed a triangle of folded binder paper into Reina's palm. "Everything you need to know is in there. Meeting times, places, phone numbers. Don't lose it and"—she glanced pointedly at Nikki, a sly smile playing on her lips, then turned back to Reina—"welcome to Comm-Comm."

Reina eyed her friend, a sinking feeling weighing down her own excitement. "B-But what about Ni—"

"Call me later," Sable said. "Bye, Nikki."

She sashayed out the door, leaving Nikki and Reina speechless in her wake. Something dribbled down Reina's forehead. Nikki pointed at it, her eyes welling with tears. Reina swallowed hard as she blotted her face with the towel.

"How . . . how could you?" Nikki sniffed, wiping her nose with the back of her hand. "You knew, didn't you?

And all along I thought we were in this together."

"We were . . . are," Reina said. "This is only the beginning. Now that I'm in, I'm going to get you in, too. I promise."

"Oh, right. Like you've got so much power."

"Nik-ki," Reina pleaded. "Don't be that way."

"Why shouldn't I? My best friend, and you couldn't even be honest. Why? Didn't you think I could take it?"

Reina shook her head. That wasn't it, exactly. Why couldn't Nikki believe that Reina was only trying to be kind?

"Well," Nikki said, "I hope you and those Pom-Commers will be very happy together. I wouldn't join that bunch of snobs if you paid me." She spun about, grabbed her backpack off the floor in the foyer, and slammed out of the house.

"Nikki, wait!" Reina called. "What about my hair?" She winced at her own self-centeredness. A sob caught in her throat, erupting like a hiccup as she turned to the stairs.

11

For the next two days, Reina hid her bushy, jet black ponytail beneath a scarf, enduring Sable's and the other girls' contemptuous stares. "Really, Reina," Sable had the nerve to say, "don't you think you'd better *do* something about your hair?"

Amanda rescued her by making a Saturday morning appointment with a hot shot hairdresser, who fringed her bangs and sides to frame her face and layered the rest into loose, voluminous waves. As her aunt paid the bill, Reina tossed her head, reveling in the swish of hair about her shoulders. "I love it," she said. "Thanks. I guess now I'm ready to go rehearse and be seen in public."

"Thank goodness. We've only got two weeks before the big day." Amanda looked at her watch. "What do you say we call Nikki? Maybe we can take her to the Sheraton for lunch, and then she can watch us rehearse."

Reina sighed. She knew what Amanda was up to, but it wasn't going to work. "How many times do I have to tell you? Nikki's still mad at me. Not that I blame her."

Amanda slipped the hairdresser a ten-dollar tip and opened the door for Reina. When she did not reply, Reina babbled on. "I've called her at least twice a day and all she says is, she's not ready to talk yet."

"That's honest."

Reina eyed her aunt accusingly. "You're saying I'm not, right?"

"No, sweetie. I just hate seeing you two like this, that's all. I hope being on Pom-Comm is worth it."

"But it *is*," Reina blurted. "It's like having instant popularity. Everybody sticks together, goes to parties, and all the neatest guys ask you out."

"I see. Guess I haven't met the lucky guy yet, huh?" Amanda unlocked the doors of her rental car.

Reina scowled as she climbed in and buckled up. "I've only been 'in' two days," she said. "What do you want?"

Amanda laughed and fired up the engine. "You're as impatient as I was, when I was in eighth grade," she said, shaking her head at the memory. "God, was I a terror."

Reina's eyes widened. "What did you do?"

" 'What *didn't* I do?' is the question," Amanda said. "I was always running around, looking for something to make me happy. Guys, booze. Even a little shoplifting. But nothing really did it. At the rate I was going, I'd have lived my whole life searching for some magical something that was never going to make me happy anyway."

"I don't get what you mean. I'm happy." Who was she trying to convince? Herself or Amanda?

Amanda pulled out into traffic, veering left onto the Beltine on-ramp. "If you are, sweetie, that's great. All I'm saying is that it didn't work that way for me." She shook her head. "Even had breast implants—not that I was all that flat to begin with. Figured *that* would do it, right? Wrong. Inside, I was still my same old miserable self."

Reina tried not to stare at Amanda's bust, accentuated by the clingy yellow muscle shirt she wore with her jeans. "You don't *seem* miserable," she said at last.

"Oh, I'm not. Don't get me wrong. But it's taken me a few wrong turns to get where I'm at. Had to learn to appreciate what's happening now, today, and stop waiting to enjoy myself until some time in the future, when all the stars align with Mars or something equally nonsensical." Amanda's expression clouded. "And as for the past . . . well, maybe it's just best to let it go. Know what I mean?"

Reina nodded as if she did. Leaving her kids—was that what Amanda meant by "wrong turns"? Or did she mean having them at all? Reina studied Amanda's profile, wondering what her cousins looked like, what they thought about their mom, how old they were, whether she'd even like them. As they neared the John Nolen Drive exit, she said, "Tell me about Ivan and Jeremy. Please?"

Amanda slowed into the cloverleaf, fishing in her

purse with one hand. At last she tossed her billfold into Reina's lap. "Look in the zippered pocket," she said. "Ivan's Tuck's age and Jeremy . . . he's eight, I think. No. Nine."

Reina pulled out two dog-eared photos, obviously taken several years ago. But there was a family resemblance in the noses and about the mouth that reminded her of Tuck. A lump rose in her throat as she struggled for words. "Did you ever . . . do they know . . . about me and the boys?"

Amanda nodded. "I'm sure their father's told them. But, well, long distance stuff is hard and letter writing is about the last thing on their list of things to do. Take it from me." She blinked quickly and fumbled for a pair of dark glasses.

"Are you okay?" Reina asked.

A quiver in Amanda's chin belied her nod. "I'm doing what I always dreamed of. Why wouldn't I be?"

Reina shrugged. "No reason." Maybe Amanda's "wrong turn" was thinking she could live out her dream at any cost. Maybe the lawsuit was just part of the price of her success. Reina toyed with the idea of mentioning it, but decided to wait. No sense putting Amanda on the defensive, especially when she was already upset about her sons. "So," she said, "are you excited about the benefit?"

"You bet. The homeless around here are going to eat well and sleep tight this winter, I'll tell you that." Amanda angled the car into a space in the Sheraton's parking lot. "But the best thing is, I've been working on a new song. With any luck, we're going to do it for the first time at the concert."

"When am I supposed to learn *that*?" Reina said, panic rising in her voice. "I'm having trouble getting all the words to the ones on the tape."

Amanda made a headband of her sunglasses, smoothing back her hair. In the sunlight, her eyes glinted like amethysts. "Don't you worry about a thing," she said, as they entered the hotel. "It's a surprise. All you've got to do is sit back and enjoy it."

From the front desk, Amanda called up to the penthouse to see if the guys were ready to rehearse. "No answer," she said. "I wonder if they're in the restaurant."

"You looking for your band?" The young desk clerk grinned shyly. "I think they're at the pool."

"Boy, would I love a swim," Reina said. Then she remembered her hair. Big deal, she thought. Who was she trying to impress?

"There's probably something upstairs you could wear," Amanda said. "A bodysuit, if nothing else."

Reina cringed at the thought of being half-naked in front of Razor. "That's okay," she said. "Maybe we ought to just get the guys and go to the studio."

"Work, work, work," Amanda teased.

Reina shrugged. "Just so I don't embarrass you. Or myself."

"You won't, as long as you kick back and go with the flow. Just pretend you're in your room."

"Oh, sure." Reina rolled her eyes. Tuck and his big mouth. She'd never be in this mess if it weren't for him.

The desk clerk pointed the way to the terrace, where they found Razor in the whirlpool and the others playing a lively game of keep-away in the pool. "Boys will be boys," Amanda said. Reina couldn't tell whether she was annoyed or amused.

Razor waved, hopped out of the spa, and came toward them, steam rising from his chest. He was wearing black-and-blue striped biker's shorts, skintight. Reina forced herself to look at his stubbly beard, at his eyes, his earrings, anything but his wet, well-muscled body.

"You look hot, love," he said.

Reina felt heat flood her cheeks, not knowing how to take his comment. Did he mean hot as in you're sweaty and need a swim? Or hot as in sexy?

"No hotter than you," Amanda said, tracing a curly tuft of his blond chest hair with her finger.

God, Reina thought. He was talking to Slate, not me. How could I be so dumb? She slouched beside her aunt, wishing she were invisible.

"You practice with that tape we brought over?" Razor asked.

Reina nodded.

"You got all the lyrics nailed down? What about the harmony?"

"I—I'm not sure, but I think so." She turned to Amanda. "You said I'll be okay, right?"

"You'll be better than okay. You'll be perfect. That's what rehearsals are for," Amanda said.

"Jesus, Slate, cut the kid some slack. Why are you making her go through with this? Can't you see she's uptight, that her heart's not in it?"

"Yes it is," Reina blurted. "I'll be fine. Really." What was the matter with her anyway? A guy came riding up on a white horse to rescue her, giving her an excuse to back out, and what did she do? Reject his help. She must be crazy. Temporary insanity; wasn't that what they called it?

"She's just a kid, for crissake. She oughta be doing homework and practicing the piano or something, not spending every last minute in the studio."

"Razor, enough."

"No. I don't think so. What if she comes unglued? What if the pressure's too much for her? Then what, huh?"

"I said chill, Jamison." Slate's voice was sharp and thin-edged, like his first name. "Her best is good enough."

"Yeah? And it's our name that's on the line if it's not."

"*My* name," Amanda corrected. "And I've had about enough of your attitude."

Razor raised his jaw, his blue eyes flashing. "*My* attitude? Take a look at yours."

"Yeah?" Slate said. "What's that supposed to mean?"

117

"The court case, man. It's really bugging me. Why aren't you sweating it? Our butts are on the line here. Or have you forgotten?"

Amanda cleared her throat. "Reina, why don't you go order a Coke or something? Put it on my charge."

"I'm not thirsty," she said. "And I know all about Joe-D Summers, if that's what you don't want me to hear."

Amanda eyed Razor accusingly, but he raised his hands and backed off. "You made the mess, Slate," he said. "You explain it."

"Whatever you heard, sweetie, it's not true."

"You're calling *Metal Mania* a liar?"

Amanda managed a nervous laugh. "As smart as you are, you'd believe a rag like that?"

"Even MTV said something about you going to court," Reina said. "Explain that."

Amanda bit her lip and sighed. "So I have to be in court. Big deal. It's a publicity thing. Joe-D's just trying to use me to promote his first tour. So he sent me a tape. It stunk, and I sent it back. End of story. It's nothing but a nuisance suit. Part of the overhead." She turned to Razor. "You've got to learn to mellow out, not take life so seriously."

"Yes, Mother." Razor's expression softened. "If you say so."

Amanda reached over, grabbed the back of his neck,

and squeezed. He ducked under her arm, dancing sideways, his fingers ripe for a tickle-attack. Reina giggled and backed out of their way, relieved to see a playful Razor. Moodiness didn't suit him, she thought.

"Tickle war!" he howled.

A couple with young children moved to chaise lounges at the far side of the pool area. The woman muttered something under her breath, while the man skewered Amanda and Razor with looks of contempt. But neither of the musicians seemed to notice as they alternately charged and parried each other's attacks. Bobby hoisted himself out of the pool, followed by Duff and Warlock.

"You in this?" Bobby asked Reina.

She shook her head and shrank farther from the action. Why not? something inside her cried. Mellow out. Don't take life so seriously. Enjoy the moment.

A waiter sidestepped Amanda and Razor and began collecting leftover plastic cups from tables around the pool. His bemused expression was a sharp contrast to the scowls from the family on the other side of the terrace.

"Reina's off limits, right?" Warlock asked Amanda.

As Razor connected with her ribs, Amanda shrieked, unable to answer.

"Jailbait's off limits for everything *but* tickling," Razor said. "Don't you guys know anything?"

Now Amanda lay on the deck, squealing for Razor to

stop, her hair splayed out around her. Bobby and the guys hovered about like vultures.

"Hey," Reina said. "Watch out. You're stepping on her hair."

"Reina, help!" Amanda was laughing so hard she could barely form the words. Kicking off her sandals, Reina charged into the melee. Bobby moved in to hold Razor's arms, allowing Reina a better shot. "Get him!" Amanda said. "Get him in the ribs!"

As she dug her fingers into Razor's sides, the drummer writhed in Bobby's grasp. He was laughing like a little kid, twisting and turning from side to side. Amanda leaped up to help her out.

"You give?" Amanda said.

Razor shook his head.

Bobby whispered something to Amanda, and her face melted into a wide grin. "Shall we? On three?"

"Whatever you say, Boss Lady."

Reina frowned, but kept tickling. Amanda counted to three, and at that instant, Bobby shoved them all toward the pool. Reina's scream echoed with Amanda's and Razor's as they hit the water in a tangled heap. She came up sputtering and laughing, her new hairdo plastered about her face like papier-mâché.

"So, love, you really want to sing with us, huh?"

Reina nodded without hesitation, self-consciously plucking at her clinging T-shirt. A prickly rush spread throughout her body.

"Then we've gotta give you a name," Razor said. "What do you say, guys? Any ideas?"

"How about just plain Rain?" Reina suggested.

"Sounds good to me," Amanda said. "What do you say we baptize you?" Reina shrugged. "Razor? You do the honors?"

The drummer grinned as he dribbled water on her face. "Rain it is," he said. "As long as you don't bring the real thing with you."

Later, as she and Amanda dripped all over the burgundy-and-gold elevator carpet on their way up to the penthouse, Reina said, "Maybe I'm wrong, but I think Razor likes me, don't you?"

"Likes as a person or likes as in——"

"Yeah," Reina said, feeling suddenly warm despite the gooseflesh on her bare arms.

"Don't want to burst your bubble or anything, sweetie," Amanda said, "but that's part of his charm—making girls think, well, you know. Truth is, he wouldn't dare touch anyone underage anymore'n he'd want some guy touching his precious little sisters."

"You're sure?" Reina wished she could tell whether she was relieved or disappointed.

"Trust me. He's a pussycat."

"Then what's he doing with a name like Razor?" The mere sound of it suggested danger, living on the edge.

Amanda laughed. "Beats Roger, doesn't it?" Turning her key, she signaled the doors to open on the exclusive penthouse floor. "I shouldn't have told you. I can see it in your eyes. I've ruined his mystique, and you're going to hate me forever."

"No I'm not." Reina tried not to think of the slashes in Razor's tight jeans or the unshaven stubble on his chin—or the way he'd looked at her when he baptized her "Rain." He was too old for her anyway; she would do better to stick to guys her own age, guys on Pom-Comm like Jamey Rhoads or Todd Boynton. "There's no way I could hate you," she said. "Not in a million, trillion years."

12

Reina floated through the next week of school on a cloud of good feelings. The rehearsals with Slate and her band had gone pretty well, and Razor finally had to agree that Reina's best *would* be good enough. Sable and the others said they loved her new hairdo and bubbled over with excitement about the upcoming benefit and their sponsorship. If only Nikki would talk to her, she thought, everything would be perfect.

The Wednesday before the concert, Sable called a special lunchtime meeting of the community action committee to discuss plans for after the concert. Reina hurried through the salad line, and, with a guilty glance at Nikki, who was sitting with some girls from her homeroom, tagged after Sable to Mr. J.'s room.

Todd was plowing through his third hamburger, at the same time trying to defend his fries from Jamey, who kept turning around to snitch them. "Hi, Sabes," Todd managed, despite his mouthful. "Rain."

She folded herself into a desk across the aisle from Jamey, and grinned back at Todd. Though he wasn't the hunk Jamey was, Todd wasn't bad in a gangly, preppy kind of way. He was bound to fill out by next year when they were freshmen.

His Adam's apple bobbed as he emptied his mouth, returning Reina's smile. Once Carrie, Ginger, and Missy arrived, Sable told everyone to hush up and get down to business.

"Okay, guys, good news," Jamey said. "We can have the party-after at *my* house." He glanced back at Mr. J., who was immersed as usual in paperwork, and lowered his voice. "My folks are in New York and left my sister in charge for the weekend, so it's no problemo."

"Cool." Todd crinkled up one eye in Sable and Reina's direction. "B.Y.O.B., right?"

"Riiight." Jamey dragged out the word. "Bring your own *bottle*, Reina," he said pointedly. "And I'll get the ice and cups and stuff."

She hadn't realized that she was frowning and quickly pulled her face into neutral. Everyone would think she was a real dork, not knowing right off what Jamey meant by B.Y.O.B. Why hadn't she remembered that she'd seen that written on a couple of party invitations that her parents had received, and that they'd brought bottles of wine? It made sense, she thought, though she, of course, would bring pop.

"Aren't we gonna have punch?" Carrie asked. "That stuff we had last time was great."

"What *was* that, anyway?" Ginger giggled.

"Wapatuli," Sable said. "You want it again?" Everyone nodded enthusiastically except Reina, who wasn't sure what wapatuli tasted like.

"I'll try to bring all the stuff, but I can't promise anything. My old man's been locking his cabinet. Hey!" Sable turned to Reina. "Maybe Slate or Razor could help us out. They *are* coming, aren't they?"

"I . . . I . . ." Reina tried without success to get the words out. She hadn't even realized that the band was invited. Why would they want to party with a bunch of eighth graders? "I didn't get a chance to ask them yet," she said. "But I will. Don't worry."

Another lie, easier this time. Reina wondered whether she had the face for it, but no one questioned her reply.

"Okay, guess that's it, then," Sable said.

"That's the way I like 'em." Jamey winked at Sable. "Short and sweet."

"Everybody meet at Jamey's after the concert. Anything else?"

Reina raised her hand tentatively. It took a long moment for Sable to notice—she'd been too busy flirting with Jamey—and in the meantime, Reina's heart had

125

begun to thrum in her chest. She willed herself to find the right words.

"Oh. Reina." Sable smiled. "Is there something else?"

"Yes. I mean . . ." Reina surveyed the others' faces, found them all expectant and friendly, and forged on. "I think we could use another person on this committee, someone who's artistic, who can help with the party."

"I think we have enough people," Sable said.

But Jamey disagreed. "I can use all the help I can get, man. Let's hear her out."

Reina let the kindness in his brown eyes buoy her faltering voice. "It's . . . Nikki Stephenson," she said. "I think she'd be a real asset."

Todd and Jamey exchanged a pointed look. A couple of the girls giggled.

"What's wrong with her?" Reina blurted. "You don't even *know* her!"

Jamey leaned across the aisle conspiratorially and slung one muscular arm over Reina's shoulder. On her face she could feel his breath, warm and reeking from a mixture of breath mints and fried onions. "It's like this, see. Her old man's a cop."

"So?"

"Do I have to paint you a picture here? Jeez. I thought you were such a brain." He released Reina but mocked her with his gaze. "The girl is trouble, and we don't need any. Got it?"

Reina bobbed her head, her lips pressed tightly to-

126

gether, and the meeting broke up. On her way out of the classroom, she felt someone sidle up and slip an arm around her waist. Todd's earnest, well-scrubbed face grinned down at her.

"Don't let him get to you." His voice felt like fingers caressing her hair. "Jamey's like that, nervous. Nikki's okay. We just can't take any chances, you know?"

Reina nodded dumbly as if she did.

"I'm looking forward to the party," he said. His hand inched upward toward her bra. "Me and you, I think we could have fun, you know?"

"Todd . . ." Reina felt her cheeks go hot; she avoided his eyes. What kind of fun did he have in mind? "Look, I've got to go. I have science, way over in D-wing—you know?—and I have to stop by my locker and—"

Todd pressed a finger over her lips. "You and me," he said. "Saturday. Count on it."

Reina blinked up at him, nudging aside a vague uneasiness she could not define. She could think of nothing to say. Absolutely nothing! Then, with a wink that made her stomach lurch, Todd turned on his heel and disappeared down the hall.

The morning of the concert, Reina dialed Nikki's number one more time. Mrs. Stephenson answered the phone. "She's in the shower, Reina. Shall I have her call you back?"

"She won't," Reina said miserably. "I wish she'd at least listen."

"I'm sorry, hon, but there's nothing—"

"Look, do you know if she's going to the concert?"

"I'm sure she wouldn't miss it. I'll tell her you asked."

After thanking Mrs. Stephenson, Reina hung up, flopping facedown on her bed. This should be the happiest day of her life, but suddenly all she felt like doing was hiding out in her room.

Probably just preconcert jitters, she thought. Or maybe she was missing Nikki. Thank goodness Tuck wasn't home to bug her and Amanda wasn't there to see her moping around. He'd harrassed their aunt into taking him with her to Elver Park to check with the roadies about the stage setup. If Amanda had her say, not even the weather would be left to chance. But with the way those clouds were boiling over in the west, all anyone could do was hope for a lucky break.

Mom knocked lightly on her door. "Come on in," Reina said, rolling onto her back.

Her mother swept aside some of Amanda's clutter and deposited a pile of clean clothes on the dresser. "All set? You nervous?"

Reina nodded miserably. "I feel like I'm going to be sick."

"Are you sure you want to go through with this? Amanda can't *make* you do anything you don't want to, you know."

"I know. But a deal's a deal." Why couldn't she just come out and admit that she was *excited* about it?

Mom fingered the red leather pants that Amanda was letting Reina wear for the concert. "These fit, huh?"

"Perfectly. And you should see the awesome lace top she gave me!" Reina jumped up to show her mother the skimpy tube top hanging in her closet.

"*Black* lace?"

"What do you think? Nikki's gonna—" She broke off, hung her head.

Mom reached out to console her, but Reina pulled away. Mom was on Nikki's side; she *had* to be. Why else would she act so weird whenever Reina mentioned Comm-Comm and the party tonight? Mom was judging her; she was sure of it.

"Look, honey, you're only thirteen. Don't you think black lace is a bit much? What would your father say?"

"How should I know?" Reina clutched the top protectively. I hardly ever see him, she said, but not out loud. "Amanda thinks it looks great, and I *am* going to wear it. I don't care what you say."

Mom raked her fingers through her hair and blew out a long breath. "Amanda. Amanda! Why do I feel like screaming every time I hear you say her name?"

"Moth-er."

"Well, what do you know? I thought you'd forgotten."

"Oh, Mom," Reina scoffed, kissing Mom's cheek

lightly. "I could never do that. Be happy for me, okay? You *are* coming to the concert."

"Wouldn't miss it," Mom said, "to see *you,* anyway."

"Don't tell me you're not even a *little* curious to catch Slate's act."

Mom grinned sheepishly. "I suppose I am. A little. It's hard to imagine. Thousands of people, all screaming for my baby sister."

Reina tried to imagine herself thinking similar thoughts about Tuck. It would be a real shock to have to admit someday that the kid was something special. She reached for the pile of her clothing and began putting it away. Mom gave her a hand.

"To be honest, I guess I *am* kind of glad you talked me into letting Mandy stay," Mom admitted at last. "It was silly of me to be so protective. Chalk it up as one of those mothering-a-first-child mistakes, can you?"

"Sure. Why not?" Reina felt glowing, expansive.

"You need a ride to Jamey's house afterward? I could poke my nose in and see if his folks have enough chaperones."

"That's okay." Reina turned away from her mother and restraightened her bed. She wondered whether the heat she felt in her cheeks was visible from where Mom was standing. "I—I think Amanda's going to take me. Thanks anyway."

She hoped that she sounded breezy, confident, like the party was no big deal. But the more she thought about it, the more she had her doubts. Why would they be so concerned about Nikki's father, unless they were planning to do something they shouldn't—like drink liquor or something? Of course. How dumb could she be, thinking bring your own bottle meant "bottle of pop"?

She glanced at her clock radio, setting butterflies free in her stomach. The old, cautious part of her wanted to confide in Mom that she wasn't sure she even wanted to go the party, while the new, courageous part wanted to find out exactly what Todd Boynton meant when he said *fun*. I've come too far to back out now, she thought. This'll be the night of my life.

Pacing across the bluish gray carpet to her desk, she hurriedly checked her purse for essentials. "Mom, no offense," she said, "but I've got to hurry. Will you drive me over?"

13

By the time they arrived at Elver Park, the stage facing the winter sledding hill was shaded by orange and blue parachutes that billowed from towering scaffolds. Chain-link fencing ran up the hillside, across the top and down the other side, enclosing the natural amphitheater. Several motor homes, to be used as dressing rooms, were parked behind the stage. Squawking microphones provided feedback for the sound engineers who bustled about, testing equipment.

"Can I go with Reina?" Brady asked.

Mom shook her head.

"No fair." Brady sulked. "Tuck gets to."

"I'm not sure where Tucker is," Mom said.

"Please, Mama?"

"No, honey. We're going to watch and listen from up on the hill, if our ears can take it."

Reina laughed as she pulled a pair of earplugs from her purse. "Thanks for reminding me."

"You wouldn't by chance have another pair, would you?" Mom teased.

Reina looked at the black rubber plugs ruefully. If Amanda saw her wearing them she might take offense. "It's okay," she said, passing them to her mother. "You take them."

After Brady and Mom had wished her good luck, Reina hustled over to Slate's trailer to get ready. Amanda was putting the finishing touches on her bright blue makeup butterfly, gilding the edges with glitter. "You all set, Rain?" she asked, talking into the mirror. "Won't be long now."

Reina nodded as she shrugged off her clothes and slipped into the lace top and leather pants.

"Want some stage makeup?"

"Sure. Why not?"

Amanda continued glossing her already-red lips, staring critically at her own reflection. When she pulled herself away at last, she draped a plastic cape about Reina's shoulders and painted a crimson butterfly that spanned her nose, eyes, and cheeks, similar to her own blue one. Together they ran through a few scales and other exercises to warm up their vocal chords. Too soon, someone knocked on the trailer door and called, "Show time!"

Reina blew out a long breath, checked her hair and makeup one last time, and followed Amanda backstage.

From the wings she saw a seemingly endless sea of faces, T-shirts, and blankets flowing uphill. Sable Murphy and Mrs. Peck, Applewood's principal, were waiting onstage by one of the mikes. When the crowd began chanting "We want Slate," Mrs. Peck raised her hands for silence.

"On behalf of the students and faculty of Applewood Middle School, I'd like to welcome you to our benefit concert for the homeless. A special thank-you to Sable Murphy and her community action committee for making all the arrangements."

Sable shook back a cascade of coppery curls, basking in the praise. When Mrs. Peck stepped aside, Sable tiptoed up to the mike, uncharacteristically shy. "It's a real honor for me to introduce Slate and her band. Come on out here, guys."

Slate pranced out, followed by Bobby, Duff, and Warlock. Razor started forward, but Reina couldn't move, couldn't swallow, could scarcely breathe, her heart was beating so fast. Instead, she just stood there, biting at a hangnail. Halfway across the stage, Razor looked back, then returned for her, taking her hand.

"Loosen up, love. Let it flow," he whispered. "Pretend they're your mirror."

Reina giggled nervously, absorbing his energy as he tugged her toward center stage.

Sable introduced each person in turn. "And as a special treat, our very own Reina Williams, from eighth-grade chorus, will be singing backup for her aunt. Everybody, I give you Slate . . . and Rain!" Sable led the applause as she edged away into the wings, grinning at Reina.

Amanda reached for Reina's hand, grabbed hold, and danced up to the two mikes at the edge of the stage. The guys faded back, connecting with their instruments. Reina loosened her mike from its pole, snapping the cord at her side. Amanda jumped and, at the instant she landed, the band exploded into an electric frenzy. Reina's mind went blank. What was the first song?

She turned to her aunt for a clue. But Amanda was no longer Amanda; with the addition of an audience, her metamorphosis into Slate was complete. It was Slate who grabbed the pole and rocked it sideways, stroking its shaft suggestively, Slate who whipped her hair in wild circles and jerked her hips at a bare-chested young man in the front row.

Reina glanced at her own mike, saw that her fingers were turning white from clutching it so tightly. "Pandora's Box," that's what the song was. She recognized it now. Finding her voice, she eased into the harmony, tried to look above the crowd lest she catch someone's eye and come unglued. The banks of speakers behind her, as well as others angled toward the band across the front of the stage, rattled her soul, set it on edge. She closed her eyes, trying to ignore the churning in her gut. When would it all be over? Why couldn't she just relax and enjoy it?

When Reina looked up, Slate was strutting across the

135

stage, twirling her mike cord like a lariat. Sweat glistened on the pale skin above her blue-sequined tube top. As she burst into the final chorus, she turned to smile encouragingly at Reina.

The next song'll be better, Reina promised herself. Just pretend this one's a dress rehearsal.

The crowd's response to "Pandora's Box" warmed Reina to the challenge. She was part of this. She *was*! All she had to do was jump in with both feet and forget everything but the moment. Forget her self-consciousness, forget about Nikki and Tuck—wherever he was —and the possibility of rain.

With the cheering and applause still rolling downhill toward the stage, Slate raced into the wings. Reina craned her neck to see what her aunt was doing. Someone was helping her change into a new top. Someone short and blonde. Could it be Nikki? From her vantage point, Reina couldn't tell, could only hope that it was. Wouldn't it be just like Amanda to try to get them back together?

Slate returned wearing a black leather halter, laced up the front with a silver-tipped thong. "Hey," she yelled into her mike, "we've got a new song. You wanna be the first to hear it?"

"Yeah," the audience roared back.

Reina swallowed hard. *Now* what was she supposed to do? Surely Amanda didn't expect her to fake something she'd never even heard before. She looked back at Razor, mounted on a platform with his drums, and tried to catch his eye. No luck. Maybe Bobby, behind her on keyboards.

"Pssst! Bobby!" she hissed. "Throw me a tambourine or something."

"Special delivery." Bobby flung the instrument at her as if it were a frisbee.

Great. How am I supposed to catch that? The tambourine sailed past her, hit a speaker on the edge of the stage, and ricocheted off. Before she could stoop to retrieve it, Tuck dove out of the wings after it.

"Here," he said, handing it over. "Good thing you didn't bend over. You'd probably rip your pants."

Reina plastered on a smile and said through clenched teeth, "Very funny. Now get out of here." For once, though, she had to admit that she was grateful for his interference. She doubted that he was far from the truth with that crack about her pants. "Hey, Tuck," she called. "Thanks."

As he retreated off stage, Slate signaled the band. Reina caught Razor's beat, tapping the tambourine against her hip. At last the lyrics blared out at her: "Don't get mad. Don't let it get you down. Don't get mad. Don't think of what you've done . . ."

Reina felt her jaw drop, her mouth go dry. Those were *her* words—her *private* words—scrawled in haste in her journal. What did Amanda think she was doing?

Reina realized that she had let her tambourine clunk to the stage; not that anyone seemed to notice. Slate's world—her fans, her band—rocked on around Reina, not missing a beat.

And Slate herself wailed on: "Look at the monkeys up in the trees. Look at the plants with their pretty leaves. They don't have to do too much, just anything they please."

Reina backed away from the screaming evidence of Amanda's betrayal, bumped into the scaffolding, turned to flee.

"Hey, Rain!" Tuck grabbed her arm. "What's the matter? Don't you want to hear the rest of it? She's using your words."

"How would *you* know, unless you were snooping in my stuff, too?" Reina tried to shake him off. "What *is* it with you people?"

Breaking free of Tuck's grasp, she hurried past Sable and a couple of other kids from the committee and clattered down the steps, bolting in the direction of her trailer. As if it were one of Slate's special effects, lightning split the sky, freeing fat raindrops to splat against her face. Soon thunder chased after her.

"Reina, hey! Wait up!"

She turned to see Sable flouncing down the stairs. "Not now, Sable." Reina waved her away.

"Just what do you think you're doing?" Sable yelled above the music. "You're going to ruin everything!"

"Me? *Me* ruin everything?"

"Get a grip, will you? You tick her off, and she won't

show up at the party. We're counting on you, Reina. I mean it."

"Oh, please." Reina rolled her eyes and turned to leave. But Sable grabbed her shoulders, and polished, dagger-filed nails clutched Reina's bare skin.

"Stop it!" Reina shrugged her off, anger on anger rising inside her. "What do you think you're doing?"

"Keeping you from being a prima donna, that's what. Makes us all look bad," Sable said. "Don't be crazy."

"I'm not," Reina snapped. "I'm having the first sane moment I've had in weeks."

"Oh, really?" Sable's voice was steeped with sarcasm. "I made you, Reina Williams, and I can unmake you real fast."

Reina opened her mouth, but words failed her. What Sable said was true—hateful, but true. Todd Boynton had never paid any attention to Reina until Sable had appointed her to Comm-Comm; *none* of the super-popular kids had, really. But a couple of words from Sable and Reina was suddenly acceptable, okay; even Todd had wanted to be with her. And why? Because of Amanda Slate, Queen of the Users. She and Sable had a lot in common.

"I'm talking to you, Williams. Either you go back out there and keep Slate happy or—"

"You can cut the ultimatums," Reina said, "because I quit. Who wants your kind of popularity, anyway?"

"You do and you know it."

"Did," Reina corrected. "But not anymore." Her sudden conviction surprised and empowered her.

Sable's dimples seemed to turn in on themselves as she stood there, glaring at Reina, rain pelting her in the face. Brown mascara streaked beneath one eye like a phony shiner.

"Excuse me," Reina said. "I've got something to do." She turned abruptly, not quite sure what that *something* was, and hustled through the hammering rain toward Slate's trailer. Damp clumps of hair hugged her cheeks and she could feel her red makeup butterfly running down her chin, but she didn't care.

Watch out what you wish for, her father always said, because it might come true. Serves me right, Reina thought. She never should have risked a real friendship for a bunch of fake ones. It wasn't worth it. If only the damage could be repaired. . . .

Her pulse was racing as much from anger as from effort as she neared the trailer. She'd done it now, ruined things with Nikki as well as making a total fool of herself, all because she had been sucked in by Amanda. Mom had warned her from the start; and yet even Mom was taken in—again—just as she'd feared.

"I could never hate you in a million, trillion years." Reina's promise to Amanda came echoing back to mock her. Hugging herself, she tried to contain the hurt and anger that were tangled up inside her. Maybe "hate" was too strong to describe what she felt right now toward Amanda, she thought. But not by much.

The trailer loomed ahead. What was she going to do? Change out of those clothes and *then* what? Hunching her bare shoulders against the rain, she rounded the corner —and collided with someone cloaked in a smelly, gray blanket.

14

"Nikki!" Reina's breath caught in her throat. "I'm *sorry*." She realized that her friend might think she was only apologizing for nearly knocking her into the mud, but when she tried to explain further, Nikki interrupted her.

"Are you okay? I was so worried when you ran off like that. You looked like you were going to barf or something." Nikki flung one end of the damp blanket around Reina, who huddled gratefully beside her. "What happened?"

"It was the song. The words. Amanda stole them."

"You sure? Who from?"

"Me." Reina locked eyes with Nikki. "Took 'em right out of my notebook. Didn't even bother to ask if she could *look*."

"That's *terrible*. What're you going to do?"

"I'm not sure." Reina opened the trailer door, relief and gratitude nudging aside her anger for the moment. Nikki was talking to her—just like that! Her friendship was more than Reina deserved. Inside, the smell of lemon air freshener competed with hair-spray ghosts and sharp cologne. "You coming?"

Nikki hesitated outside the trailer. Rain pelted the metal roof and splashed around her muddy sneakers. "You sure you want to be seen with me?"

"Every day, all the time," Reina said. She tugged on Nikki's hand, and Nikki did not resist.

"What about Sable?"

"Who?" Reina batted her false eyelashes, feigning ignorance.

But Nikki wasn't smiling. "Stop kidding around. I'm serious."

"So am I. Sable and those guys are history."

"Yeah? As of when?"

"Five minutes ago."

"Well, that's convenient." Nikki bit her lip. "Sorry. I didn't mean to sound so—"

"Yes you did, but I don't blame you. It's true, though. Sable lit into me back there, and I told her where to get off. Who needs her?"

"Right. What does anyone need with popularity?" Nikki swiped a tissue off the dresser and began dabbing at Reina's runny butterfly.

"Trust me, Nik, it's overrated."

"Yeah?"

"Yeah. From the outside it looks great, I'll give you that. But looks aren't everything. It's what's real that counts."

Nikki sighed, flopping down on the day bed. "You sound just like my mother, you know that?"

Reina laughed. "I tried to get you voted in. I really did, but . . ."

"But what?"

"They thought you'd rat to your dad about their parties."

Nikki shook her head in apparent disbelief. "That's it? Oh, Reina, but that's great! It's not about me at all." She jumped up, flung her arms around Reina.

"Forgive me, Nikki?" Reina hunched forward, felt Nikki's head bob against her shoulder. She blinked back tears, then broke away, feeling awkward. "You want to help?"

Nikki nodded. "Anything. You name it."

"Help me get the rest of this junk off my face, will you?"

"Sure. But what about the show? You going back out there?"

Reina shook her head. "There's no way I'd give her the satisfaction."

Nikki found some cold cream and slathered it over what remained of the butterfly. Together they tissued off the red makeup. Then Reina peeled away the leather pants and lace top, hurriedly donning her T-shirt and jeans.

"What are you going to do now?"

Reina shrugged, feeling her anger creep back out of hiding. "I don't know. I'm so mad, I can't even think straight. You know what this means, don't you? Amanda *did* take Joe-D Summers's lyrics, just like it said in your magazine. I bet you any money. If she'd steal from her own niece, what's to stop her from doing the same thing to a total stranger?"

"Not a thing. Look," Nikki said, "Slate can change outfits by her own dumb self. She doesn't need me."

"So she *did* do something right today." Reina remembered her earlier suspicions about Amanda trying to get them back together. "At least we're talking again."

"You got that right." Nikki gathered up the blanket and offered it to Reina. "What now? Anything else I can do?"

Reina shook her head. "Thanks anyway. I just need some time to think. Can I call you later?"

Nikki nodded. "You sure you're okay?"

"No." Reina laughed. "But if I wait until I *am,* I'll be waiting forever."

"Isn't that the truth? It's like that bumper sticker we saw at the mall, remember? The one that said 'TODAY IS NO DRESS REHEARSAL. IT'S THE REAL THING. ACT NOW.' "

"I could use one of those plastered across my mirror,"

145

Reina said, draping Amanda's clothes neatly over the back of a chair and grabbing her purse. "Catch you later, okay?"

Leaping out of the trailer, she turned back to wave, hunching her shoulders against the rain.

"You're gonna get soaked again," Nikki called.

"You're right. But it beats hanging around here." Reina twirled around, her face turned to the sky, letting the rain wash it. Already her T-shirt was beginning to cling to her skin, but she didn't care. If the only way out of this place was through the rain, so be it.

Slate's new song ended at last in a flurry of drumbeats. Undampened by the change in weather, the audience's cheers pursued Reina into the woods. She was running now, her heart beating a joyful cadence of *Nikki-Nikki-Nikki* as her footfalls snapped twigs and pummeled the wet grass. Beyond the trees lay a meadow, golden brown and thirsty, soaking up the storm. Lightning crackled overhead; thunder boomed in its wake. As Reina pressed on, the strap of her shoulder bag grazed the stitch in her side.

The Williamses' subdivision sprawled beyond the park, black clouds thrown over it like a discarded cape. The streets were licorice snakes, glossy and twisting. Reina slowed to a walk as she headed down Muir Field Road. What was she going to do about Amanda?

A horn honked behind her, startling her from her thoughts. She turned to see Mom behind the wheel, and

Brady rolling down the window. "Come on, honey, get in," Mom said.

Her first instinct was to say no, but she was tired of running, tired of pushing her mother away. Mom was not her enemy—never had been—and Reina knew that she of all people would understand how Reina was feeling right now.

"Why did you run away, Reina?" Brady asked, peering at her over the seatback. "You were doing good."

"I—I realized something," she said. "And then it wasn't fun anymore."

"Oh." Brady faced forward again, apparently satisfied with her explanation. And though Mom's frown reflected in the rearview mirror, she didn't question Reina further until they were home. Pushing a dog-eared copy of *Fox in Socks* at Brady, she shooed Reina upstairs.

"What *did* happen, honey? You're not sick, are you?"

Reina shook her head. She explained about the lyrics Amanda had taken from her journal, and about the plagiarism lawsuit. "She's supposed to be in court on Thursday," she said. "Maybe I ought to go testify against her myself."

Mom's fingers caressed the ruffles on the canopy over Reina's bed. "I was so afraid something like this would happen," she said. "Why do I persist in believing she can really change?"

"It's not your fault, Mom."

"No wonder she wanted to make up. Her whole

world's caving in, and all she's got is herself."

To blame, Reina thought bitterly. She glanced about her room at the fallout of Amanda's visit—clothes heaped everywhere in little piles, bottles of exotic skin-care lotions strewn about the dresser, their caps off or askew. If only she could make it all go away.

"Well . . ." Mom shrugged awkwardly. "I'll be downstairs if you feel more like talking later."

Reina nodded and began stripping off her wet clothes. As she did, she glimpsed the corner of her notebook, peeking out from under the mattress. Funny she hadn't noticed it before. Her breath caught as she pulled it out and cradled it against her bare chest. As if that could keep it, keep *her*, safe from future violations.

Her mirror bounced back reflections of a victim, huddled, clutching, helpless, and of black-and-blue slats of sky framed between her miniblinds. She imagined Nikki's bumper sticker at eye level: "TODAY IS NO DRESS REHEARSAL. IT'S THE REAL THING. ACT NOW!" She stood up taller, shook back her damp hair. Act now. First things first.

After locking her door, she rummaged around for a new hiding place for her journal. At last she slipped it behind her headboard and got dressed.

After a quick trip to the basement, she returned with Amanda's suitcase. She folded tops and pants and skirts into precarious stacks, then arranged them neatly in the great leather valise. Tucking the teddies, bras, and pantyhose into the empty spaces, she arranged boots and spiky high heels in a jigsaw-puzzle layer across the top. It was hard to believe that Amanda still had more stuff at the Sheraton.

At last she folded the denim LAS VEGAS jacket and laid it to rest with all the solemnity of a funeral wreath. Her fingers stroked the sequined cityscape, then abruptly let go. With a sniff, she stepped back to appraise her efforts.

Downstairs a door slammed. Reina opened hers a crack so she could hear, so she could be ready.

"Hey, Mom, we're back!" Tuck hollered. "What's with Reina?"

"Please wait for me in the family room," Mom said.

"Gimme a break. Brady's reading *Fox in Socks* out loud. Again!"

"Tucker, please." Groaning in protest, Tuck plodded down the hall. "Well, well, well. If it isn't Slate," Mom said. "Concert over so soon?"

"We cut it short." Amanda's terse reply drifted up the stairway. "On account of the rain."

"Oh, right."

"Where's Reina? She okay?"

"Funny you should ask," Mom said.

Reina's pulse quickened as footfalls drummed toward her room. She dived to close and lock the door. Moments later the knob rattled.

"Hey, sweetie," Amanda said, "what gives?"

Reina rolled her eyes. "As if you didn't know."

"Come on. Let me in. We'll talk."

"We'll talk all right," she said, and grudgingly opened the door. She could feel the tension in her forehead, the scowl dragging down the corners of her mouth.

"You get cold feet or something?" Amanda reached out to touch her, but Reina pulled away, exposing the packed suitcase on the floor behind her. Amanda stared at it, her expression a mask. "What's all this? I don't understand."

"Does stealing stuff out of my journal sound familiar? Dear *Aunt* Amanda." Her tone dripped with sarcasm. "I trusted you."

Amanda blinked, her lips parted, a sculpture of innocence. "I—I thought you'd be pleased. Flattered. I wanted to surprise you."

"Some surprise," Reina said. "That was private. You had no right."

Amanda hung her head, shook it slowly. "I'm so sorry. It was just . . . there . . . and good. Just what I was looking for. But I—I never thought you'd mind. I just assumed . . ."

"I suppose you thought Joe-D Summers would be flattered, too?"

Amanda flinched as if she'd been slapped. She pressed her lips together, blinking quickly as tears welled in her eyes. Reina hugged herself, hugged back the rage.

At last Amanda spoke. "Joe-D's got nothing to do with

this. He's just trying to . . ." She looked as trapped as a spider in her own web. "What can I do? Just tell me, sweetie. Is there anything . . . any way . . . I can ever make this up to you?"

"Maybe you should just go to Chicago. Do what you've got to do. You have what you came for."

"What's that supposed to mean?"

"Mom. At least she's talking to you again."

"In a manner of speaking." Amanda shook her head, still eyeing the floor. "She could have really *been* somebody, you know? She had it all—brains, looks. Everything but balls. Guess I inherited those, huh?"

Reina massaged the tightness in her chest, keeping her voice steady. Amanda had balls all right, if ever a woman could. "Mom *is* somebody," she said. "We all are."

Amanda shook her head. "She chickened out, my big sister. Got married, settled."

"So?" Reina said. "There's nothing wrong with getting married. Nothing hard about it, either. It's *staying* married that's the challenge."

Amanda hung her head. "I guess I deserved that." When she gazed at last into Reina's eyes, her own had turned thoughtful. "At least *one* good thing came out of Emmy's marriage," she said.

"Yeah? What's that?"

"You."

Reina swallowed hard. What about Tucker and Brady? What about Ivan and Jeremy? Boys, all of them. Just like

151

Slate's band. And despite their messes and pranks and irritating ways, boys were special, too. It was a shame that Amanda couldn't see that, Reina thought.

She eyed a spot on the carpet. Shoe polish, maybe. She had to get that out before it set. When she looked up again at Amanda, her aunt's arms were extended hopefully. Reina hesitated, then saw the pain in her aunt's eyes as she quickly withdrew the gesture.

"I won't produce the song, sweetie. I promise. It will just . . . disappear." She turned to the suitcase, her gaze falling on the denim jacket. "Please," she said, "at least accept *this*." Activating the lights, she danced the flashing bulbs before Reina's eyes.

The memory of a happier day, full of trust and new discoveries, reared up from the outrageous garment. Even her fight over it with Mom seemed a good thing, a sign of testing her own wings, of becoming her own person, and yet . . . Reina tried on the idea of wearing it, imagined the kids' reactions at school—Sable's, especially —that used to matter so much. She realized that she was shaking her head.

"I don't want it," she said. "It wouldn't feel right."

"Please?" Amanda sounded like a whiny child used to getting her own way.

"No, thank you."

"You're sure? You are, aren't you?" Amanda's brave, bittersweet smile did not melt as she cinched up her suitcase. "Better call my lawyer, huh? I can see I've got

152

some rethinking to do before Thursday morning."

"Glad to hear it." Reina hesitated, biting her lip. "Whatever happens, at least let us know, okay?"

"You still mad?"

Reina nodded. "But I s'pose that's a good sign."

"It is?"

Reina nodded again. "Daddy always says you don't bother getting mad at somebody unless you care about 'em."

"Wise man, your daddy." Amanda smiled hopefully. "Think I can try again?" she asked, opening her arms toward Reina.

With a will of their own, "Reina's feet shuffled forward; her arms reached out to embrace Amanda stiffly. How fragile and birdlike she felt! How different from the tough persona of Slate, the heavy metal rock star.

"Well," Amanda said, releasing her abruptly, "I guess this is it." She hefted the valise and ducked quickly out of the room.

Reina watched from her doorway as Amanda descended the stairs, and when her aunt turned back to look at her one last time, Reina couldn't help but notice the feisty, upraised angle of Amanda's jaw. She's tough all right, Reina thought. Whatever the verdict, she'll be okay.

Tucker and Brady thundered down the hall below her, firing questions at Amanda about why she was leaving. Reina grabbed a bottle of stain remover and a brush from the bathroom, closing the door on her aunt's replies.

Among the lavender and pink throw pillows on her bed she spied Chopsie, limp and lovable and visible at last after having been buried amid Amanda's belongings.

When Dad gets home, Reina thought, he's going to put in a new lock for me, the key kind. Right away, no excuses.

She wanted to call Nikki; it felt like eons since they had really talked. But first she knelt over the spot in her carpet. She had to get rid of it, banish all traces, get her room back to normal. Squirting the brush with cleaner, she began scrubbing, back and forth, back and forth, throwing her whole body into the effort, and as she did, her tears worked free at last.

By the time she rocked back on her heels to inspect her work, sunlight split the miniblinds and painted stripes across the rug. Stroking her hand against the nap, Reina saw its true color, as if for the first time, and wondered, Had it always been slate blue?